ชาว

7-ค

THE SEVENTH KANSAS CAVALRY:
ITS SERVICE IN THE CIVIL WAR.

AN ADDRESS

BEFORE THE STATE HISTORICAL SOCIETY, DECEMBER 2, 1902.

By S. M. FOX,

First Lieutenant and Adjutant.

ALSO,

A BRIEF NARRATION OF THE FIRST EIGHT KANSAS REGIMENTS.

STATE PRINTING OFFICE,
TOPEKA, 1908.

1282

STORY OF THE SEVENTH KANSAS.

Reprinted from eighth volume of the Kansas Historical Collections.
(Notes by the Secretary.)

An address before the State Historical Society, December 2, 1902,
by S. M. Fox,* First Lieutenant and Adjutant.

THIS is not intended to be a history, but is a sketch, based, from a lack of sufficient records, on a memory which at times may be at fault. From the conditions, the story can but be rambling and incomplete. The history of a cavalry regiment that nearly every day during its four years of active service was in the saddle would fill many volumes with stories of adventure and hardship and then be a tale half told.

At the beginning of the civil war Kansas had just been admitted as a state, the machinery of government was hardly in working order, and the people were very poor; yet when the call of the president for troops came the response was immediate, and always in excess of every demand. Eight regiments were organized and placed in the field during the year of 1861. Much confusion existed in the organization of these regiments, resulting from the action of the War Department at Washington in giving Senator James H. Lane authority to raise troops

---

* SIMEON M. FOX was born in Tompkins county, New York, August 28, 1842. When he was eleven years old he moved with his family to Elmira. He was educated in the high school at Elmira and the Genessee college at Lima. His father came to Kansas in 1855, and located at Highland; the mother came later, and the son remained East attending school. In the spring of 1861, upon the close of school, the son came to Kansas, immediately enlisting in company C, Seventh Kansas regiment. He served nine months as a private, then was made a corporal, a regimental sergeant-major, and then first lieutenant and adjutant, which place he held until mustered out. At the close of the war he settled in Manhattan, and engaged in the book business. He was appointed adjutant general of the state in 1895, serving during the administration of Governor Morrill, and was reappointed by Governor Stanley in 1899, serving six years.†

The Kansas regiments during the civil war have a disjointed and very imperfect record of their service. There is a wide-spread impression that their service was practically limited to patrolling or bushwhacking along the border, or leisurely camping on the plains. Because of the controversy between Gov. Charles Robinson and Senator James H. Lane, the organizations of some of the regiments read like chaos. The directors of the Kansas State Historical Society, prompted by the military pride of the people and their observation of the value of patriotic ancestry, determined to gather the story of the state's soldiery as complete as possible, in justice to the descendants of those who made a record as brilliant as that of any of the nation's defenders. Adj. Gen. S. M. Fox, who served with the Seventh Kansas during its entire enlistment and was mustered out as regimental adjutant, at the solicitation of the Society, prepared "The Story of the Seventh Kansas," herewith published, which shows a strenuous service at the front, and which it is hoped may be an incentive and guide to the members and friends of other regiments. The Kansas State Historical Society has the story of the Nineteenth, Twentieth, Twenty-first, Twenty-second, and Twenty-third, also well told. See volume 6, Historical Collections. For further sketch and muster-roll of the Seventh Kansas, see Adjutant General's Report, reprint 1896.—G. W. M.

and organize regiments of volunteers in Kansas independent of state authority. The first two regiments were, however, practically organized before Senator Lane appeared, armed with a brigadier general's commission, to begin his independent recruiting. These two regiments had been ordered on the 23d of May to rendezvous, one at Leavenworth and one at Lawrence. The regiment rendezvoused at Leavenworth was mustered into the United States service on May 30 as the First Kansas volunteer infantry, under the command of Col. George W. Deitzler, and immediately ordered into the field. The secretary of war, deeming the draft too heavy for so young a state, hesitated about mustering in the second regiment. When, however, General Lane arrived in Kansas, on Friday, June 7, Governor Robinson sent his quartermaster general, George W. Collamore, post haste to Washington, who after persistent urging finally secured the following order.

WAR DEPARTMENT, June 17, 1861.

To his Excellency Charles Robinson, Governor of Kansas:

SIR—This department will accept, for three years or during the war, two regiments of volunteers from Kansas, in addition to the one commanded by Colonel Deitzler and mustered already into service, said regiments so accepted to be the ones commanded by Colonels Phillips and Mitchell, respectively; and the mustering officer ordered by the adjutant general to muster them into the service is hereby directed to make such requisition as may be necessary to supply them with arms and ammunition, clothing, etc., they may require, and also to supply any deficiency that may exist in Colonel Deitzler's regiment.   SIMON CAMERON, *Secretary of War.*

The Second Kansas volunteer infantry was mustered into the United States service for three years at Wyandotte immediately thereafter, under the command of Col. Robert B. Mitchell. Many recruits had enlisted in this regiment with the understanding that it was for three months' service; they expressed dissatisfaction, and the regiment was finally ordered to be mustered out on October 31, 1861, but nearly all its members soon after joined other regiments. The Second Kansas cavalry, organized later, May 7, 1862, was practically a new organization, although commanded by Colonel Mitchell and retaining in its ranks a number of the officers and men of the old Second Kansas infantry.

The Third and Fourth Kansas volunteers were regiments of mixed arms, and were organized by General Lane. These two

regiments, with the Fifth Kansas cavalry, constituted what was known as "Lane's brigade." The Third was mustered into the United States service at Mound City on July 24, 1861, under the command of Col. James Montgomery. This regiment took the place of the third regiment authorized by the secretary of war in the order of June 17, previously quoted. The Fourth Kansas volunteers was mustered into the United States service about the same time, under the command of Col. William Weer. The Fifth Kansas cavalry was mustered in under the command of Col. Hampton P. Johnson, who was killed in actiᵣn at Morristown, Mo., on September 17, 1861, and was succeeded in command by Col. Powell Clayton.

The Sixth Kansas cavalry was mustered in at Fort Scott on September 10. It was commanded by Col. William R. Judson.

The Seventh Kansas cavalry was mustered into the United States service as a complete organization at Fort Leavenworth on October 28, 1861, under the command of Col. Charles R. Jennison.

The Eighth Kansas volunteer infantry was organized with eight companies during October, 1861, and was commanded at its organization by Col. Henry W. Wessels.

It will be remembered that in June the secretary of war was hesitating about authorizing a second regiment, for fear of making too great a draft on a young and sparsely settled state, yet four months later eight regiments had been organized and were in the field, and all this was done without one dollar being offered or paid by the state to secure enlistments. . I have given this brief sketch of the eight regiments recruited in Kansas in 1861 as preliminary to the story of the Seventh Kansas, and to show the patriotic conditions that existed when this regiment was organized. All these regiments helped to. make history. and have left records of unfading glory. The First and Second Kansas fought on the bloody field of Wilson Creek, and their heroism there has given a luster to the name of Kansas that time can never dim. One hundred and six men was the death record of the First Kansas alone during that terrible day, and this regiment marched off the field in perfect order when the battle was lost. The Second Kansas, although not suffering so great a mortality, left a no less brilliant record for bravery and discipline. The Third and Fourth Kansas regiments were never complete or-

ganizations, but, with the Fifth Kansas cavalry, did excellent service along the Missouri border, and their presence there undoubtedly saved Kansas from rebel invasion when, after the dearly bought and doubtful victory at Wilson Creek, the Confederate general, Sterling Price, marched north to Lexington, in September, 1861. The Third and Fourth Kansas volunteers were broken up in February, 1862, and assigned to other regiments. The infantry companies were consolidated, and became designated thereafter as the Tenth Kansas volunteer infantry; the cavalry companies were transferred to the Fifth, Sixth and Ninth Kansas cavalry, and helped to complete the organization of those regiments. The Fifth and Sixth Kansas cavalry regiments served to the end of the war in Missouri, Arkansas and the Indian Territory with great credit, and took part in all the principal battles west of the Mississippi fought after Wilson Creek. The Eighth Kansas infantry served in the Army of the Cumberland. The regiment lost heavily at Chickamauga, and was one of the first regiments to reach the summit of Missionary Ridge, in the famous charge of Wood's division at the battle of Chattanooga.

In the absence of records, it is difficult at this late date to know under whose authority some of these regiments of 1861 were organized. Governor Robinson resented the interference of the War Department in sending General Lane to Kansas to raise troops independent of the state government, and when General Lane began to recruit, and usurp what the governor considered his constitutional rights, he went ahead and raised troops himself and ignored Lane as far as possible. The governor also made matters as uncomfortable as possible for him; he started a fire in his rear by appointing Fred P. Stanton to fill the vacancy assumed to have been created in the senate when General Lane was confirmed as a brigadier general, and the senator general was given much trouble to maintain his seat. The First, Second, Seventh and Eighth regiments were clearly raised under state authority, and the Third and Fourth regiments by General Lane; the Fifth cavalry, while a part of Lane's brigade, was practically organized under state jurisdiction; the Sixth cavalry originated under authority of General Lyon, who authorized the organization of several companies for the defense of the border near Fort Scott; additional companies of the Sixth were organized by order of Major

Prince. This action seems to have been approved by Governor Robinson, and the Sixth was practically organized under state authority.

It was natural that a state made up of the hardy settlers who came to Kansas to make it a free state should be patriotic. The men all had convictions, and they knew that the war was inevitable, and expected when the time came to take a hand in the game. Military companies began to report to the state government as soon as Kansas became a state, and before the end of June, 1861, there was scarcely a hamlet that did not have its military organization that met nearly every night for drill. Leavenworth city alone had twenty-three companies; Atchison and Doniphan county and the settled counties to the westward were organized and asking for arms. The border counties from Wyandotte to Bourbon kept their old companies, organized for the protection of the border, alive, and organized others in addition. All through the state, as far west as Junction City, these companies were drilling and preparing for the trouble to come. Many of these organizations enlisted in the United States service in a body and were the nucleus of the permanent volunteer regiments. Whenever a company so enlisted, another company was organized to take its place at home. There is one thing that must be said: many of the soldiers in the Kansas volunteer regiments came from other states, directed here by motives that were various, but this class was mostly made up of men of abolition belief who wanted to help strike a blow at slavery in the name of Kansas. They left states where large bounties were being offered and enlisted in Kansas, a state too poor to pay an additional bounty, and composed of a class of citizens so patriotic that no such inducement to enlist was ever required.

It will be observed that the Kansas regiments were numbered consecutively, without reference to the arm of service they represented.

About the 1st of August, 1861, Governor Robinson gave authority to Dr. Charles R. Jennison to raise a regiment of cavalry. Something of a glamour surrounded Jennison in those days; he had been conspicuous as a leader in the early days of border troubles, and his "jayhawkers" had inflicted damage on the pro-slavery sympathizers that ranged all the way from blood to loot; indeed, he carried the latter to such an extent that the pedigree of most Kansas horses, it was said,

should have been recorded as "out of Missouri by Jennison."
So when Jennison began to raise his regiment the organization became immediately known as "the jayhawkers," a name
that followed through its whole history, as the war records
will show. Much conjecture as to the origin of the word "jayhawker" has been indulged in; one story is that it was a
modification of "gay Yorker," an appellation applied to Doc-
tor Jennison when he first came to Kansas, he having been
of sportive proclivities and hailing from the Empire state.
There are always persons who take a great deal of trouble to
explain or account for a very natural or commonplace thing.
The predatory habits of the jayhawk would indicate that the
name as applied to Jennison's men was singularly appropriate,
and one need not speculate as to what suggested the application. The "jayhawkers" did not certainly originate then,
for as early as 1849 a little band of Argonauts from Illinois,
who made the overland journey to California, called themselves "the jayhawkers"; they were lost in Death Valley, and
the thrilling story of their suffering and final rescue has often
been told. I have seen it somewhere, but I cannot now recall

---

1. The most interesting party that ever crossed the plains. the discoverers of
Death Valley, of silver in Nevada and of the great niter deposits in the desert east
of California, were the "jayhawkers of '49." The party was made up at Galesburg,
Ill., from which place they started April 5, 1849. They crossed the Missouri river
at Omaha. Since 1872 the survivors of this party have held annual reunions. The
first was held that year in Galesburg. Ill.. and the last one was at Lodi. Cal., February 4, 1903. On the 4th of February, 1850, John B. Colton. who now resides in
Kansas City, Mo.. saw the first sign of vegetation, and on that day thirty-two of the
thirty-six emerged from Death valley terribly emaciated wrecks. Seven of the party
are now known to be alive. The Historical Society has had letters from three of
them. one being from Mrs. Juliette W. Brier, the only woman in the party, now past
ninety years old. When the party reached a Spanish ranch. big, strong men were
nothing but wrinkled skin clinging over visible skeletons. Their teeth showed in out-
line beneath clinging parchment cheeks. At the last reunion but three attended,
Mr. Colton. from Kansas City, a gentleman from San Jose, and the hostess, Mrs.
Brier. Mr. Colton has a newspaper scrap-book, containing as much as 3000 columns
of reading-matter, about the "jayhawkers of '49," and yet the world cannot get
away from the impression that the word originated in a Kansas raid on Missouri.
John B. Colton, of Kansas City. Mo.. in a letter, gives the origin of the word:
"For the information of the Bostonese. who is endeavoring to fix the origin of the
word 'jayhawker,' I will say that it was coined on the Platte river, not far west of
the Missouri river, in 1849, long before the word 'Kansas' was known or heard of.
I cannot tell him why, but I was there. Some kind of hawks, as they sail up in the
air reconnoitering for mice and other small prey, look and act as though they were
the whole thing. Then the audience of jays and other small but jealous and vicious
birds sail in and jab him, until he gets tired of show life and slides out of trouble in
the lower earth. Now, perhaps this is what happens among fellows on the trail—
jaybirds and hawks enact the same role. pro and con—out of pure devilment and to
pass the hours of a long march. At any rate. ours was the crowd that created the
word 'jayhawker,' at the date and locality above stated. Another thing: in the
mountains and mines of California, in those early days. words were coined or born,
climatic surroundings materially contributing. The words were short, like the latter-
day 'tenderfoot'; 'shorthand' meant a line, a sentence, and perhaps a whole page. I
have heard a word that meant a whole lifetime to the other fellow. Now, when these
Argonauts of early times returned to the states, those shorthand words clung to

where, that the name was of common application in Texas during the struggle for liberty, but of this I am not sure.

Colonel Jennison was commissioned as such on September 4, 1861, and recruiting began immediately. Burning placards were posted in the villages offering inducement in way of proposed equipment that would have made every man a portable arsenal. The recruit, in imagination, saw himself bristling with death and desolation, mounted on an Arabian barb, breathing flame as he bore his rider to victory. All this was in strong contrast to the pitiful equipment that was at first in reality issued,

The field and staff of the Seventh Kansas at organization was as follows:

Colonel	Charles R. Jennison.
Lieutenant-colonel	Daniel R. Anthony.
Major	Thomas P. Herrick.
Major	Albert L. Lee.
Adjutant	John T. Snoddy.
Quartermaster	Robert W. Hamer.
Surgeon	(vacancy).
Assistant surgeon...............	Joseph S. Martin.
Chaplain	Samuel Ayers.
Sergeant-major	William A. Pease.
Quartermaster sergeant	Eli Babb.
Commissary sergeant	Lucius Whitney.
Hospital steward	John M. Whitehead.
Hospital steward	James W. Lansing.
Chief bugler....................	George Goss.
Chief bugler....................	John Gill.

them and were distributed among the surrounders, and they took them up and perpetuated them. Possibly an early-timer, in the troublous times of new Kansas, when they were settling difficulties in promiscuous ways, may have known or heard the word 'jayhawker' from the far West, and knew it was a winner, and so adopted it as a talisman. So far as Kansas is concerned, the word was borrowed or copied; it is not a home product. I knew many of the leaders in jayhawker times of early Kansas '50's, and have met them at Leavenworth and other points frequently in those days."

Mr. U. P. Davidson writes from Thermopolis, Wyo.: "In answer, I will state that our company was made up from schoolboys at Galesburg, Ill. We formed an order of our own. One of our party suggested the name of 'jayhawk,' so that was adopted. Our company has gone by that name ever since." A few days out from Salt Lake the jayhawkers left a large party and took a different course. In a day or so more they were joined by Rev. Mr. Brier, wife, and three little boys. When Mrs. Brier reached the ranch at the end of their march through Death Valley the Spanish women cried piteously and hugged her to their bosoms as though she were a child. Mrs. Brier writes that "they (the company) took upon themselves the name Jayhawker when they started for California."

Company A was organized the last part of August, 1861, principally in Doniphan county, although the northern tier of counties supplied recruits from as far west as Marshall. The original officers were:

Captain .... Thomas P. Herrick.
First lieutenant................... Levi H. Utt.
Second lieutenant................. Thomas H. Lohnes.

The company was recruited by Captain Herrick, of Highland, in conjunction with Lieutenant Utt, of White Cloud, and was mustered into the United States service at Fort Leavenworth August 27, 1861. When the regiment was organized, on October 28, Captain Herrick was made a major, and Lieutenant Utt was promoted to captain, and Sergt. Aaron M. Pitts was commissioned a first lieutenant to fill the vacancy. Second Lieutenant Lohnes remained in his original grade until his resignation, February 13, 1862. Major Herrick became lieutenant-colonel on September 2, 1862, and colonel on June 11, 1863. Captain Utt had served under General Lyon in Colonel Blair's First Missouri infantry and was a proficient drill-master. He molded the company, and it was through his first training that the company became and always remained the most efficient and reliable organization in the regiment; and there is no disparagement to the other companies in saying this; all were good, but company A was a shade better. Let me say here that the military nomenclature of the civil war differs from the present; the word "troop" as now applied was not then used; "company" was, at the beginning of the war, applied alike to cavalry and infantry; later, in 1863, the name "squadron" became the designation of a company of cavalry. The word "squadron" as applied to cavalry, as the equivalent of "battalion" as applied to infantry, is of much later date.

Captain Utt was one of the most fearless men that I ever saw; when in the greatest hazard he seemed entirely unconscious of danger. He lost a leg at Leighton, Ala., April 2, 1863, while charging a battery with his mounted company; his horse was killed under him. As soon as the stub healed sufficiently, he outfitted himself with a wooden leg and came back to the command of his company. He was promoted major November 17, 1864, which rank he held until finally mustered out with the regiment. Although a young man, the name "old timber-toes" became his familiar appellation.

First Lieut. Aaron M. Pitts was appointed captain of company D October 3, 1862; the vacancy created was filled by the promotion of Sergt. Bazil C. Sanders to first lieutenant. Second Lieutenant Lohnes resigned February 13, 1862, and Jacob M. Anthony was appointed to the vacancy from civil life. On the promotion of Captain Utt to major, Lieutenant Sanders, who had gallantly commanded the company while Utt was disabled by wounds, became captain, and under his command the company always maintained its reputation for efficiency. Lieutenant Anthony was promoted to captain and assigned to company I on May 16, 1863, and Sergt. Dewitt C. Taylor was promoted to the vacancy. Sergt. Henry C. Campbell was appointed a first lieutenant to fill the vacancy created by the promotion of Sanders.

All these officers proved themselves to be brave and efficient. Lieutenant Lohnes was, however, a deserter from the regular army, but no question as to his bravery was ever raised; for cold-blooded nerve he was not often equaled. After his resignation he followed the regiment as far as Rienzi, Miss. From there he went back to Kansas and indulged in a little "jayhawking" on his own hook. He was captured, but while under guard at White Cloud, one cold winter night, when all the guards had come in to the fire in an old building where he was confined, he raised up as if to stretch himself, and, with a remark about hard luck, suddenly jumped through the window, carrying away sash and glass. The guard rushed out, but their prisoner had vanished. He was heard from in 1865, and was then living in Nova Scotia.

Company B was organized by Capt. Fred Swoyer, of Leavenworth; it was composed of men recruited in Leavenworth and Atchison counties, except about thirty men brought from Chicago by Lieut. Isaac Gannett. The company was recruited during September, 1861, and partially organized with two officers, First Lieut. Fred Swoyer and Second Lieut. William S. Moorhouse. Early in October, when Lieutenant Gannett arrived with his recruits from Chicago, the organization was completed, with the following officers:

Captain .... Fred Swoyer.
First lieutenant................. Isaac Gannett.
Second lieutenant............... William S. Moorhouse.

Captain Swoyer commanded the company until he was killed,

January 3, 1863. He was succeeded by Capt. William S. Moorhouse, promoted from second lieutenant. Lieutenant Gannett was absent from the regiment on staff duty during most of his term of service and lost out on promotion in consequence. Moorhouse was succeeded as second lieutenant by Charles L. Thompson, advanced from first sergeant. Lieutenant Thompson deserted February 18, 1863.

Captain Swoyer was a man of great physical courage, but exceedingly reckless. In the winter of 1861-'62 he did a little steeple-chasing down Delaware street, in Leavenworth, and while putting his horse over a sleigh loaded with cord-wood, standing across the street, the animal fell and broke the captain's leg. He limped through the rest of his life. His death was the result of his recklessness, but he was brave and patriotic and did splendid service while he lived. After the death of Captain Swoyer the company was temporarily commanded by Capt. Bernard P. Chenoweth, of the First Kansas infantry, who was with the company for a short time; after his departure Moorhouse was made captain, as above stated. Captain Chenoweth was a gallant officer, who had done splendid service at Wilson Creek with his regiment. He was very punctilious, and exceedingly neat in his dress; he always wore a black regulation hat with a long white feather trailing down his back, but you can be assured that, like the white plume of Navarre, it would always be seen dancing in the forefront of battle when the fight was on. Moorhouse became captain April 22, 1863, and Chenoweth returned to his old regiment. Moorhouse commanded the company most efficiently until he was mustered out, March 7, 1865.

Sergt. John A. Middleton, a member of company B, who deserted at Germantown, Tenn., in February, 1863, gained a later notoriety; he was the desperado, "Doc" Middleton, who terrorized a portion of Nebraska some twenty years ago.

Company C was recruited in Leavenworth city by its first captain, William S. Jenkins. About twenty-five men recruited in Doniphan and Brown counties completed the organization. Recruiting began September 5 and the organization was perfected at Kansas City on October 10, with the following officers:

Captain .... William S. Jenkins.
First lieutenant.................. Francis M. Ray.
Second lieutenant................ James Smith.

Captain Jenkins commanded the company until his promotion to major, May 27, 1863. He was promoted to lieutenant-colonel March 21, 1864, and resigned November 14 of same year. Lieutenant Ray resigned December 8, 1861, and was succeeded by First Lieut. James D. Snoddy, appointed from civil life. Lieutenant Snoddy was later temporarily transferred to company G, and left the service in December, 1862. Snoddy was succeeded by Lieut. John A. Tanner, promoted from second lieutenant of company F. Lieutenant Tanner resigned July 23, 1863, and was succeeded by the promotion of Second Lieut. Bayless S. Campbell. Captain Jenkins was succeeded by Capt. James Smith, promoted from second lieutenant July 1, 1863. Lieut. Bayless S. Campbell, promoted from sergeant, filled the vacancy created by the advancement of Smith; when Campbell was promoted to first lieutenant he was succeeded by Second Lieut. John H. Wildey, promoted from first sergeant.

Captain Jenkins was an efficient officer and deserved his promotions. Lieutenant Ray and First Sergt. John H. Gilbert were the original drill-masters of the company. They had both served in the regular army, and were efficient, and soon had the company whipped into excellent shape. Lieut. James Smith, later captain, was a native of the East Tennessee mountains, and had an intense hatred for a rebel. He was a big, awkward fellow, with very light hair, which he always wore close cropped; he never escaped the name of "Babe," given him at his first enlistment. He was perfectly fearless and would fight an army rather than retreat, and, when he held the command of the company, had always to be watched and ordered back in a most peremptory manner or he was liable to stay too long. He would have died any time rather than surrender, as the story of his death will attest. After his discharge from the service he went to southern Kansas, where he jumped, or rather took possession of, a claim deserted by the original preemptor; a party of men who considered him an interloper rode out to drive him off. He did not drive, and when they opened fire he promptly returned it, and killed two of their number before he himself fell. As one of the posse bent over him to ascertain if he was dead, he suddenly raised his pistol hand and sent a bullet through the brain of his inquisitive enemy, and with a look of grim satisfaction joined him on his unknown journey. Poor old Jim! His men always loved him, and when he was twice de-

prived of promotion by the appointment of officers from outside the company over him they made it so uncomfortable for
the intruders that they were glad to be transferred to more
agreeable surroundings. Lieutenants Campbell and Wildey
were brave men and made good officers. Lieutenant Campbell
commanded the artillery detachment attached to the regiment
in 1863. Ex-Gov. E. N. Morrill was a member of this company during the first year of its service. He served as company commissary sergeant until he was promoted to captain
in the subsistence department.

Company D was recruited in Bureau county, Illinois, and
vicinity. It was organized at Wyanet, by Capt. Clark S.
Merriman, in August, 1861. The company had not been assigned when it came to Fort Leavenworth on escort duty, and
was induced to cast its fortunes with Jennison's regiment,
then organizing at that post. The company was made up of
a fine lot of men and was always considered a great acquisi-
tion. The officers at organization were:

Captain .... Clark S. Merriman.
First lieutenant................. Andrew Downing.
Second lieutenant................. Isaac J. Hughes.

Captain Merriman was promoted to major October 3, 1862,
and resigned July 13, 1863. Lieutenant Downing remained
with the company until the close of his original term of service, September 27, 1864. Lieutenant Downing was writing
poetry then, as he is to-day, and I have a printed sheet of his
poems of 1861, written under the *nom de plume*, "Curley Q.,
Esq." Second Lieutenant Hughes was not a success, and resigned June 2, 1863. Hughes was at first familiarly known
as "Shang Hai," which was soon abbreviated into "Shang."
He once had an exceedingly narrow escape from death. At
Coffeyville, Miss., he was in command of his company, and,
when it was dismounted and ordered on the firing line, sent it
in under command of First Sergeant Hinsdale, while he personally took charge of his lead horses in the rear. The gallant
Hinsdale was killed. The vacancy created by the promotion
of Captain Merriman was filled by the advancement of Lieut.
Aaron M. Pitts, of company A, who commanded the company
until its final discharge. When Lieutenant Downing was mustered out, First Sergt. William Henry was promoted to first
lieutenant to fill the vacancy. No appointment was made to

fill the vacancy created by the resignation of Second Lieutenant Hughes. Lieutenant Henry was an exceptionally fine officer, absolutely fearless, and, although a boyish-appearing, smooth-faced young fellow, had a remarkable control over men.

Company E was originally organized at Quincy, Ill., in the month of August, 1861, by Capt. George I. Yeager. The members of the company were mostly from Chicago. The company arrived at Fort Leavenworth on September 22, and moved immediately to Kansas City, where it joined the other companies of the regiment recruited up to date, that were temporarily stationed there. The original officers were:

```
Captain ...................... George I. Yeager.
First lieutenant................. Charles H. Gregory.
Second lieutenant................ John Noyes, jr.
```

Captain Yeager became very unpopular with his men, and was forced to resign on October 8, 1861, and First Lieut. Charles H. Gregory was commissioned captain, and First Sergt. Russell W. Maryhugh was appointed first lieutenant, on October 18, 1861. Captain Gregory was promoted to major April 8, 1864, and Second Lieutenant Noyes was promoted captain to fill the vacancy on May 19, 1864; the vacancy in grade of second lieutenant was never filled. First Lieutenant Maryhugh was mustered out October 12, 1864, by reason of the expiration of his term of service, and was succeeded by the promotion of Corp. Edwin T. Saunders, of company A. Captain Gregory was a man of the greatest bravery and dash and had the knack of doing just the right thing at just the proper time. His gallantry produced brilliant results and much of the credit earned by the regiment was due to him. Noyes and Maryhugh were both sturdy and reliable soldiers. Lieutenant Saunders was little more than a boy, but he never knew what fear was.

Company F was organized by Capt. Francis M. Malone, of Pana, Ill., in September, 1861. The company was recruited largely in Christian county and vicinity. Captain Malone brought his men to Kansas and joined Jennison's regiment in October, 1861. The original officers of the company were:

```
Captain ...................... Francis M. Malone.
First lieutenant................. Amos Hodgeman.
Second lieutenant................ John A. Tanner.
```

Captain Malone was promoted to major August 12, 1863, and to lieutenant-colonel November 19, 1864, and was in command of the regiment during the most of its last year's service. Lieutenant Hodgeman was promoted to captain and assigned to company H June 23, 1863. Second Lieut. John A. Tanner was promoted to first lieutenant of company C, and First Sergt. Edward Colbert was promoted to second lieutenant to fill the vacancy October 31, 1862, and promoted captain October 26, 1863, and was in command of the company until its muster-out. First Sergt. John Clark was promoted to first lieutenant October 26, 1863, and resigned February 15, 1865. First Sergt. John W. Moore was appointed first lieutenant July 17, 1865, and was mustered out with the regiment. The vacancy in the grade of second lieutenant, occasioned by the promotion of Lieutenant Colbert, was never filled.

Captain Hodgeman was a brave officer and was killed in action. Captain Colbert had previously served in the regular army and was a good officer and most excellent in the field.

Company G was recruited in Linn county, Kansas, and vicinity, by Capt. Edward Thornton, and was mustered into the United States service on October 12, 1861, with the following officers:

Captain .... Edward Thornton.
First lieutenant.................. David W. Houston.
Second lieutenant................ Christopher C. Thompkins.

Captain Thornton commanded the company during its full term of service. First Lieutenant Houston was promoted captain of company H September 30, 1862, and promoted lieutenant-colonel July 1, 1863. Lieutenant Thompkins resigned February 1, 1862. Sergt.-maj. Harmon D. Hunt was promoted to first lieutenant, to fill the vacancy created by the promotion of Lieutenant Houston. Lieutenant Hunt resigned November 30, 1864, and was succeeded by First Lieut. Zachariah Norris, promoted from second lieutenant January 17, 1865. The vacancy in the grade of second lieutenant created by the resignation of Lieutenant Thompkins was filled by the appointment of Richard H. Kerr from civil life. Lieutenant Kerr was dismissed from the service November 24, 1862, and the vacancy created was filled by the promotion of Corp. Zachariah Norris, who was promoted to first lieutenant as above.

Private William A. Pease was appointed second lieutenant to fill the vacancy. Captain Thornton was a generous, whole-souled man, and made an excellent company commander. Lieut. Zach. Norris had been a soldier in the old Second Kansas infantry, and had been severely wounded at the battle of Wilson Creek.

Company H was organized by Capt. Marshall Cleveland, of jayhawker fame, and was mustered in at Fort Leavenworth on September 27, 1861, with the following officers:

Captain .... Marshall Cleveland.
First lieutenant.................. James L. Rafety.
Second lieutenant................ Charles E. Gordon.

The original company was largely made up of members of Cleveland's old band of jayhawkers, that had operated along the Missouri border. Captain Cleveland was one of the hand-somest men I ever saw; tall and rather slender, hair dark, beard dark and neatly trimmed. He was very neat in his dress and his carriage was easy and graceful. As a horseman he was superb. A stranger never would get the impression from his appearance that he was the desperate character that he was. His real name was Charles Metz. He was a native of New York state, had been a stage-driver in Ohio, and had served a term in the Missouri penitentiary. After his gradua-tion from this institution he had for a time called himself "Moore," but later settled down on to the name "Cleveland." He did not remain with the regiment long; he could not endure the restraint, and one evening at Fort Leavenworth the cul-mination came. The regiment marched out for dismounted dress parade; Colonel Anthony was receiving the salute and, as the regiment was formed, took occasion to censure Captain Cleveland for appearing in a pair of light drab trousers tucked in his boot-tops. Cleveland immediately left his station in front of his company and advanced directly towards the colonel; all expected bloodshed, but it only culminated in a few characteristic and pointed remarks on the part of the two officers immediately involved, and Cleveland passed on. He mounted his horse and rode away to Leavenworth city, and immediately sent in his resignation, and we saw him no more. He soon gathered a band of kindred spirits about him and be-

gan his old trade of jayhawking.[2] He was quite impartial in
his dealings with rebels and Union men at the last, and if
there was any question he took the benefit of the doubt. He
made his headquarters at Atchison and eluded for a time all
attempts to capture him; once or twice he captured the posse
sent out after him and, after taking their horses and arms,
sent them home on foot, as may be supposed, somewhat crest-
fallen. He finally ran up against the inevitable while trying
to escape across the Marais des Cygnes, when pursued by Lieutenant Walker with a squad of company E, Sixth Kansas cavalry; he was shot and killed by a sergeant. He sleeps peacefully in the cemetery at St. Joseph. The headstone which
marks his grave bears this gentle epitaph:

> "One hero less on earth,
> One angel more in heaven."

Cleveland was succeeded in command of the company by
Capt: Horace Pardee, appointed from civil life. Captain Pardee led a strenuous life during the few months he was with the
regiment. He was wounded at Columbus, Mo. He resigned
May 15, 1862, and was succeeded by Capt. James L. Rafety,
promoted from first lieutenant. Rafety was dismissed August
31, 1862. Capt. David W. Houston, promoted from first lieutenant of company G, was next in succession, and commanded
the company until his promotion to lieutenant-colonel, July 1,
1863. He in turn was succeeded by Capt. Amos Hodgeman,

2. JOHN JAMES INGALLS published in the *Kansas Magazine*, April, 1872, an article
entitled "The Last of the Jayhawkers." Two paragraphs will suffice:

"The border ruffians in '56 constructed the eccaleobion in which the jayhawk was
hatched, and it broke the shell upon the reedy shores of the Marais des Cygnes. Its
habits were not migratory, and for many years its habitat was southern Kansas; but
eventually it extended its field of operations northward, and soon after the outbreak
of the war was domiciled in the gloomy defiles and lonely forests of the bluffs whose
rugged bastions resist the assaults of the Missouri from the mouth of the Kaw to the
Nebraska line.

"Conspicuous among the irregular heroes who thus sprang to arms in 1861, and
ostensibly their leader, was an Ohio stage-driver by the name of Charles Metz, who,
having graduated with honor from the penitentiary of Missouri, assumed, from pru-
dential reasons, the more euphonious and distinguished appellation of Cleveland.
He was a picturesque brigand. Had he worn a slashed doublet and trunk hose of
black velvet he would have been the ideal of an Italian bandit. Young, erect, and
tall, he was sparely built, and arrayed himself like a gentleman, in the costume of
the day. His appearance was that of a student. His visage was thin; his complexion
olive-tinted and colorless, as if slicked over with the pale cast of thought. Black,
piercing eyes, finely cut features, dark hair and beard, correctly trimmed, completed
a *tout ensemble* that was strangely at variance with the aspect of the score of disso-
lute and dirty desperadoes that formed his command. There were generally degraded
ruffians of the worst type, whose highest idea of elegance in personal appearance was
to have their moustaches dyed a villainous metallic black, irrespective of the consideration whether its native hue was red or brown. It is a noticeable fact that a
dyed mustache stamps its wearer inevitably either as a pitiful snob or an irreclaim-
able scoundrel."

promoted from first lieutenant of company F, July 23, 1863. Captain Hodgeman died of wounds received at Wyatt, Miss., October 16, 1863. Capt. Charles L. Wall, promoted from first lieutenant April 6, 1864, was Captain Hodgeman's successor, and commanded the company until its final discharge.

The first lieutenants of the company were: James L. Rafety, promoted and dismissed as above; John Kendall, promoted from second lieutenant May 15, 1862, and dismissed the service November 22, 1862; and Charles L. Wall, promoted from second lieutenant September 1, 1862. Lieutenant Wall having been promoted to captain, was succeeded by the promotion of Lieut. Samuel N. Ayers from first sergeant, May 28, 1864. Lieutenant Ayers resigned March 20, 1865, and First Sergt. Wallace E. Dickson was promoted to fill the vacancy, and held the rank until the muster-out of the company.

The second lieutenants were: Charles E. Gordon, who resigned February 11, 1862; John Kendall, promoted as above; Charles L. Wall, promoted from sergeant May 15, 1862, and later promoted to first lieutenant and captain; Samuel R. Doolittle, promoted from first sergeant September 1, 1862, and resigned March 3, 1863. Doolittle was succeeded by Joseph H. Nessell, promoted from sergeant April 8, 1863. He was dismissed the service April, 1864, and the vacancy was never filled.

Company H was made up of splendid fighting material, but did not have the proper discipline at first. After Cleveland's resignation, many of his old men deserted and joined the band their old leader was organizing. When Blunt was made a brigadier-general, Jennison, who was an aspirant for the promotion himself, was highly wroth, and made an intemperate speech while in camp at Lawrence, during which he practically advised the men to desert. That night a number of men, principally from company H, took his advice and disappeared. Jennison himself sent in his resignation, which was promptly accepted on May 1, 1862, and the regiment was relieved of a worthless officer. Houston, Hodgeman and Wall were fine officers and brought the company out in excellent shape. Some of the best and most daring men of the regiment were in this company. Capt. Amos Hodgeman did much to discipline and make company H what it eventually became. He was a man of great bravery, and I believe was liked by his men. He was dark, with a countenance that gave him an almost sinister ap-

pearance; he rarely smiled and did not talk any more than necessary. He was mortally wounded October 10, 1863, while leading a charge at Wyatt, Miss. A severe fight was in progress between the cavalry forces under General Hatch and General Forrest. As we were forcing the rebels back, they made a determined stand around a log house on a ridge. A charge had been made and repulsed, and Captain Hodgeman was leading the second assault when he fell, mortally wounded; he died on October 16, 1863. Hodgeman county was named after him. He was born in Massachusetts, and when the war broke out was a carpenter and builder in Leavenworth city.

There is a pathetic story connected with his life that may here be told. After he joined the regiment he married a pretty young woman who served drinks in a Leavenworth beer hall. In the spring of 1863 he brought her to the camp, at Corinth, Miss., and she remained there for a number of weeks. The wives of a number of the other officers were there, but Mrs. Hodgeman made no attempt to push herself into their company; she seemed contented with her husband's society, and busied herself in taking care of his quarters. They were very fond of each other, and that was enough. The camp became liable to attack any day from Forrest, and the women were sent north. After Captain Hodgeman's death, she came to the regiment dressed in deep mourning, and went out with her husband's old company under a flag of truce, secured his body, and took it away for burial. Soon after she entered a military hospital at Cincinnati, Ohio, as a nurse. She was never very robust, but she steadily performed her duties, growing a little less strong each day. She was always patient and gentle, and worked on until she could work no more. She did not have to wait long before death came to her as her reward. Poor Kitty Hodgeman! There are heroes who deserve to be "enskied and sainted" other than those who, striving for principle, go down in the forefront of battle.

One of the members of company H has since become famous —W. F. Cody, "Buffalo Bill." He entered as a veteran recruit, and was mustered out with the regiment.

Company I was recruited by Maj. Albert L. Lee in Doniphan county. Major Lee lived at Elwood, opposite St. Joseph, and a number of recruits came from that city. Lee was made a major at the organization of the regiment, and on May 7,

1862, was promoted to colonel. The company was recruited in October, and was mustered into the United States service October 28, 1861, with the following officers:.

Captain	John L. Merrick.
First lieutenant	Robert Hayes.
Second lieutenant	Edwin Miller.

Capt. "Jack" Merrick resigned November 27, 1862, and was succeeded by Capt. Jacob M. Anthony, promoted from second lieutenant of company A. First Lieut. Robert Hayes died of disease at Corinth, Miss., September 20, 1862, and was succeeded by the promotion of Second Lieut. William Weston. Second Lieut. Edwin Miller resigned September 27, 1862, and First Sergt. William Weston was promoted to the vacancy. When Weston became first lieutenant the grade of second lieutenant remained vacant. Company I was steady and reliable at all times, and did splendid service; it was made up of a lot of unpretentious men who came promptly when needed and remained until orders directed them otherwise. Capt. Jack Merrick was something of a character; he was somewhat Falstaffian in his proportions, and used to wear a pair of big cavalry boots that slopped down about his heels. His oft-repeated phrase, "If the court knows herself, and I think she do," rings in my ears yet. Captain Anthony, who succeeded him, was a brother of Daniel R., but he had been molded from more plastic and tractable clay. He had courage and staying qualities, and made up in persistency what he lacked in aggressiveness. He was an excellent company commander, and I believe that he, of all the officers appointed from civil life who came to the regiment after it went into the field, overcame the resentment of the men and served through to the end.

Lieutenant Weston was a quiet soldier who did his duty always, and the regimental commander always knew that if he was sent to accomplish a purpose it would be done, if within the limits of possibility.

Company K was originally organized at Jefferson, Ashtabula county, Ohio, by John Brown, jr., on September 6, 1861. Captain Brown sent the company on to Fort Leavenworth under the command of First Lieut. Burr H. Bostwick, and remained for a time in Ohio to finish the recruiting. Company K reached Fort Leavenworth on November 7, 1861, and was

mustered into the United States service on November 12.[3] The officers at the original muster were:

Captain .... John Brown, jr.
First lieutenant................. Burr H. Bostwick.
Second lieutenant............... George H. Hoyt.

Captain Brown was the son of John Brown of heroic fame. He was with the company very little, on account of ill health; he soon found that he could not perform the service, and resigned May 27, 1862. Second Lieut. George H. Hoyt was made captain to fill the vacancy; he was jumped over a man better qualified in every respect for the command of the company. Hoyt had the good taste to resign on September 3, 1862, and Bostwick was given his deserved promotion. He commanded the company during the remainder of its term of service. The vacancy in the grade of second lieutenant was filled by the appointment of Fred W. Emery from civil life, May 27, 1862. Emery was promoted first lieutenant and adjutant October 30 of same year, and Sergt. Thomas J. Woodburn was promoted to fill the vacancy in the company. Lieutenant Woodburn was killed in action at Coffeyville, Miss., on November 5, 1862. Sergt. William W. Crane was appointed second lieutenant August 15, 1863, and first lieutenant September 30 of same year, the vacancy in the grade of second lieutenant remaining unfilled.

As may be supposed, company K was made up of abolitionists of the intense sort. I believe that it was this company that brought the John Brown song to Kansas; at least, I had never heard it until they sang it, immediately after their arrival. For a while after the company joined the regiment the men would assemble near the captain's tent in the dusk after "retreat" and listen to the deep utterances of some impassioned orator; the voice was always low and did not reach far beyond the immediate circle of the company, who stood with heads bent, drinking in every word. The speaker always closed with "Do you swear to avenge the death of John Brown?" and the answer always came back low and deep, "We will, we will"; then would follow the John Brown hymn,

---

3. A dispatch from Washington tells of the death of Frederick C. Peck, January 24, 1908, in his sixty-eighth year. He had been a chief in the pension bureau for twenty years. Frederick C. Peck came to Kansas from Ohio with Capt. John Brown, jr., in company K. His residence is given as Riceville, Ohio. He enlisted September 6, 1861, and was discharged for disability November 6, 1862. He enlisted as a private, was promoted sergeant November 12, 1861, which rank he held until his discharge.

sung in the same repressed manner, but after the last verse of the original song was sung it would be followed by a verse in accelerated time, beginning with "Then three cheers for John Brown, jr." This almost lively wind-up of these nightly exercises had the same effect on me as the quickstep that the music plays immediately on leaving the enclosure after a soldier's burial. At first the whole regiment used to gather just outside of the sacred precincts and listen, but soon it ceased to attract, and the company itself became too busy avenging to hold their regular meetings.

Of the officers, Bostwick, Woodburn, Emery and Crane were all efficient. Captain Brown never had the opportunity to show the stuff he was made of, his broken health forcing him to resign very soon. Lieut. Tom Woodburn was a brave, dashing fellow, with a clean-cut, attractive face; he went gallantly to his death leading his company at Coffeyville. Lieut. Fred Emery was a man of unusual ability, and had a strong personality that would even override the regimental commander if his opinions went counter to the adjutant's idea of matters in question. He was promoted to the staff department as assistant adjutant general June 30, 1863. Captain Bostwick was an energetic officer and fearless of danger. He was quick to execute a command, and in case of a sudden attack his company was under arms and out to the defense before any other. Captain George H. Hoyt was a combination of ambition and cruelty; posing as a defender of John Brown at his trial at Harper's Ferry, he went after and secured a commission as an officer of the young John Brown's company. He did nothing to deserve the promotion that he received over a better and more deserving man. The company and regiment were well rid of him when he resigned.

These ten companies as described made up the Seventh Kansas cavalry. At the beginning of the civil war the cavalry regiment of the United States army was a ten-company organization, and it was only after the war had progressed a year or two that the twelve-squadron organization was adopted. The Seventh Kansas, although making repeated efforts, was never able to secure the privilege accorded to the other cavalry regiments from the state, of recruiting the two additional squadrons. The numbering of the regiment as the "Seventh" was not done until in the spring of 1862; previous to that time

the regiment designated itself as the "First Kansas cavalry." In December, 1861, the governor, in making his report to the War Department, designated it as "1st Calvary or 6th Regiment," and he designated Judson's regiment, which became finally the Sixth Kansas cavalry, as the "Seventh regiment." Some time during the spring of 1862 the numbering was definitely fixed and Jennison's regiment became the Seventh and retained that designation thereafter.

In the beginning I gave the field and staff as first organized. Many changes occurred during the career of the regiment. Colonel Jennison performed some acts worthy of commendation, conspicuous among which was his resignation. Jennison was succeeded by Col. Albert L. Lee, advanced from major. Some trouble arose at the time of Colonel Lee's appointment, from an act of Lieutenant-governor Root, who, assuming that he was governor in the absence of Governor Robinson, who had gone beyond the limits of the state, issued a commission to Charles W. Blair, as colonel of the Seventh. Governor Robinson himself, immediately after his return, issued a similar commission to Colonel Lee. Colonel Blair appeared at Fort Riley, where the regiment had been stationed, one morning just as the command was forming for its march to Fort Leavenworth, preparatory to moving south. He assumed command of the regiment, put it in motion toward the Missouri river, and promptly disappeared. The day following Colonel Lee met the regiment and assumed command also; he rode with it a short distance and finally ordered it into camp. He had "assembly" sounded, and, after he had a made a speech to the men, vanished also. Colonel Lee went directly to Washington and submitted his case to Attorney-general Bates, who decided the contention a few weeks later in his favor.

Colonel Lee ranked from May 17, 1862; he was promoted a brigadier-general November 29 of the same year. He won his star at Lamar, Miss., where the Seventh Kansas alone, although two miles from any supports, attacked Colonel Jackson's Confederate cavalry division over 4000 strong, and routed them with great loss. Colonel Lee was succeeded by Col. Thomas P. Herrick, who had passed through the successive grades of captain, major, and lieutenant-colonel. Colonel Herrick was not an officer as impetuous as Lee, but he was brave, and a safe and judicious commander and an excellent disciplin-

arian. He was a lawyer of fine ability, and was in demand
when a detail for court-martial service was required. He died
of cholera not long after his discharge from the military service. After Colonel Herrick left the service, the regiment was
commanded by Lieut.-col. Francis M. Malone until the final
discharge of the command.

Lieut.-col. Daniel R. Anthony commanded the regiment during its early service; Colonel Jennison was nominally in command part of the time, but he was too busy playing poker over
at Squiresville, or elsewhere, to find time to take the field in
person. Colonel Anthony was equal to the occasion, and the
regiment led the strenuous life while he exercised his authority. He resigned September 3, 1862. The succeeding
lieutenant-colonel was David W. Houston, who retired from
the service on account of disability February 1, 1864. Maj.·
William S. Jenkins was promoted lieutenant-colonel March
27, 1863, and resigned November 14, 1864. Lieut.-col. Francis
M. Malone was next in succession, and held the grade until
the regiment was discharged.

The majors who served with the Seventh Kansas were,
Daniel R. Anthony, Thomas P. Herrick, and Albert L. Lee,
accounted for above. Maj. John T. Snoddy followed next; he
was promoted from adjutant July 22, 1862, and resigned
March 6, 1863, on account of ill health. He died April 24,
1864. Next in succession was Clark S. Merriman, promoted
from captain of company D; he resigned July 13, 1863, and
was succeeded by William S. Jenkins, who was promoted to
lieutenant-colonel March 21, 1864. Maj. Francis M. Malone
came next; he became lieutenant-colonel November 19, 1864.
Majs. Charles H. Gregory and Levi H. Utt were the last, and
were mustered out with the regiment. Gregory was an officer
·of especial brilliancy and dash, and performed many acts of
distinguished bravery. He had splendid judgment, and never
failed of success when he made an attack. It was to his dash
the regiment owes much for its victory over Jackson at Lamar.
Major Utt was also brave to a fault; he had no conception of
what fear was, and yet was watchful and a safe officer. He
lost a leg at Leighton, Ala.

Lieut. John T. Snoddy was the first adjutant. He was succeeded by Lieut. Fred W. Emery, who was promoted to the
staff department. The vacancy was not regularly filled, but
Lieut. Harmon D. Hunt acted until the promotion of Sergt.-

maj. Simeon M. Fox to the position, which he filled until the
regiment was discharged. Lieut. William O. Osgood was battalion adjutant for a time, but was mustered out by order of
the War Department in the fall of 1862.

The quartermasters of the regiment were, Robert W. Hamer,
Ebenezer Snyder, and James Smith, who filled the position
successively in the order named.

Lucius Whitney was the original commissary, and held the
position during the full term of service.

Maj. Joseph L. Wever was the first regular surgeon; he resigned June 7, 1864, and was succeeded by Maj. Joseph S.
Martin, promoted from assistant surgeon.   Martin was the
original assistant surgeon, and, on promotion, July 18, 1864,
was succeeded by Lieut. Joel J. Crook.

The chaplains were Samuel Ayers, who resigned August 31,
1862, and Charles H. Lovejoy, appointed April 19, 1863, and
discharged with the regiment.

When Price moved north to the capture of Lexington Mo.,
all available troops were pushed forward to the defense of
Kansas City.   Companies A, B and C being organized, were
hurried to Kansas City from Fort Leavenworth and remained
there until all danger had passed; they were later joined by
company E and, I believe, by some of the other companies as
rapidly as organized.   After Price had begun his retreat these
companies were returned to Fort Leavenworth by river transport.   October 28, 1861, all companies having been recruited,
the regiment was regularly organized.   Company K was not
present, but was on its way from Ohio; it arrived November 7
and was assigned its designating letter.   The regiment was
mounted and equipped at once; the equipment was disappoint-
ing, however, as pertains to carbines; companies A, B and H
received the Sharp's carbine, but the other companies had at
first to content themselves with nondescript weapons that
ranged from the obsolete horse-pistol mounted on a temporary stock to the Belgian musket.   Later the Colt's revolving
rifle was issued to the seven companies, and it was not until
the last year of the war that the regiment was uniformly
outfitted with the Spencer carbine.   The Seventh Kansas, as
soon as the equipment was completed, marched south and
went into camp near Kansas City, companies A, B and H on

the Majors farm, located about four miles southeast of Westport, and the rest of the regiment on O. K. creek.

On the evening of November 10 Colonel Anthony received information that the rebel colonel, Upton Hayes, was in camp on the Little Blue, about thirteen miles out. He at once moved, with parts of companies A, B and H, and surprised the camp early on the morning of the 11th. The enemy was driven out and the camp captured, with all the tents, horses, and wagons. The rebels, however, retreated to an impregnable position among the rocks beyond and made a stand; they numbered nearly 300 and Colonel Anthony had but 110 men. The attempt to drive the enemy from the rocks cost the jayhawkers nine men killed and thirty-two wounded. The camp was destroyed and our boys retreated, bringing off the captured property. The fighting was most desperate and lasted several hours, and although not entirely successful caused Up. Hayes to retire from the neighborhood, and, moreover, showed the fighting qualities of the regiment to be all that could be desired.

From Kansas City the regiment marched back towards Leavenworth and went into camp at a point about nine miles south of the city. This camp was named "Camp Herrick," after the major. Here the first pay was received. Camp was broken soon after, and the regiment returned to the vicinity of Kansas City and went into camp on the Westport road, just north of the old McGee tavern, and scouted the country in that section. Independence was raided and the citizens were given a little touch of the misfortunes of war. Colonel Anthony made a characteristic speech to the citizens, who had been rounded up and corraled in the public square.' The secession spirit, which had been rampant in Independence since Price's raid on Lexington, was much subdued after this expedition. The regiment moved from Kansas City and was camped at Independence, Pleasant Hill, and West Point, in the order named, scouting and making it uncomfortable for the guerillas in the vicinity. On December 24 the command moved from West

4. Britton, in his "Civil War on the Border," attempts to give an account of this raid on Independence. He fixes the date as the latter part of September, and places the command of the expedition under Colonel Jennison, whom he accredits with the speech at the court-house square. The facts were that the Seventh Kansas was not organized at that time. The raid was towards the middle of November, and under the command of Col. D. R. Anthony. Colonel Anthony made the speech at Independence. Colonel Jennison was not present, nor was he in personal command of the Seventh Kansas (or First Kansas cavalry, as then known) while doing active service in Missouri at any time while he was colonel of the regiment.

Point to Morristown, arriving there after night. It was a
bitter cold day, and the march was made in the face of a
blinding storm. Camp was made in the snow and an uncomfortable night was passed. The winter of 1861-'62 was spent
in tents. New Year's day was devoted to a raid out into the
vicinity of Rose Hill and Dayton. The latter town was burned.

On January 5, 1862, a foray was made into Johnson county,
Missouri, by a battalion under command of Major Herrick.
His force was composed of companies A, B, D and F. The
battalion went into camp at Holden and detachments were
sent out to scout the country in different directions. Company A went to Columbus and camped for the night; a considerable force of the enemy was in the neighborhood, but as
Captain Utt was on the alert they did not attempt to attack.
After company A had moved out company D came up and
occupied the town. As Captain Merriam was leaving the village his company was fired on from ambush and five men
killed, and he was compelled to retreat. Soon after, Captain
Utt, learning of the disaster, returned to Columbus, buried
the dead, and burned the town. He remained in the vicinity
until nightfall, but the rebels failing to attack, he moved with
his company back to Holden. Two days later the entire detachment returned to Morristown.

On January 31 the Seventh Kansas marched to Humboldt,
Kan., where camp was established until March 25. On this
date the regiment broke camp and moved to Lawrence, remaining there until April 22. From Lawrence the command
proceeded, via Topeka and route south of the Kaw, to Fort
Riley, where it was joined by Mitchell's brigade of infantry,
cavalry, and artillery. The orders were to remove to New
Mexico as soon as grass had started sufficient for grazing. On
May 18, however, this order was countermanded and the entire brigade ordered to march to Fort Leavenworth and from
thence to move by river transports to Pittsburg Landing,
Tenn. The command embarked at Fort Leavenworth on May
27 and 28, and was carried as rapidly as possible to its desti-
nation. The landing was made at the Shiloh battle-ground
and the boys were permitted to see the wreck and desolation
that resulted from the great battle recently fought.

A pleasant incident occurred here that will always cling to
my memory. While at Morristown, Mo., the regiment had
been brigaded with a battalion of the Seventh Missouri in-

fantry, under Major Oliver. While coming up the Tennessee river our leading transport, "The New Sam. Gaty," had joined in a race with another river steamboat, and our boys in their zeal had burned up all their "sow-belly" to assist in getting up steam. When we arrived at Pittsburg Landing we were hungry and out of rations. An infantry soldier on the levee, who was of the Seventh Missouri and one of our old comrades, discovered this condition and immediately ran down the levee yelling that the jayhawkers were there hungry and out of grub. In half an hour a formal invitation to dinner came, and the entire boat load was fed. The Seventh Missouri had divided their rations and I have no doubt went hungry in consequence.

As our army had occupied Corinth on May 30, the pressing need for cavalry had passed and the regiment was once more ordered on board transports and carried down the river and around to Columbus, Ky. From Columbus it moved south on June 7, as a guard for the working parties occupied in repairing the Ohio & Mobile railroad to Corinth. While performing this duty the regiment was camped for a time at Union City, and while there Colonel Anthony, in the absence of Gen. R. B. Mitchell, was in temporary command of the brigade. During this time he took the opportunity to issue his celebrated order, dated June 18, 1862, and containing the following language: "Any officer or soldier of this command who shall arrest and deliver to his master a fugitive slave shall be summarily and severely punished according to the laws relative to such crimes."

General Mitchell, on returning, ordered Colonel Anthony to rescind this order. Colonel Anthony refused, stating that as he had been relieved from command he had no authority to countermand a brigade order. General Mitchell then said hotly, "I will place you in command long enough for you to rescind it." Anthony then asked, "Am I in command of the brigade?" General Mitchell replied, "Yes." Then, said Colonel Anthony, "You, as an officer without command, have no authority to instruct me as to my duties." If this order was ever rescinded it was not Colonel Anthony who did it. It will be remembered that the government was handling the question of slavery very gingerly in the early part of the war, and every encouragement was being given Kentucky to maintain her attitude of non-secession. Colonel Anthony was deprived

from command, but remained with the regiment until September 3, 1862, when his resignation was accepted. Major Herrick succeeded Colonel Anthony and commanded the regiment until Colonel Lee returned to relieve him.

There was an incident consequent on this order of Colonel Anthony's that should not be lost to history. The regiment was marching towards Corinth when, on July 3, late in the afternoon, tired and dusty, it entered Jackson, Tenn. Gen. John A. Logan was just convalescing from wounds received at Shiloh, and was in command of this post. While the regiment was halted in a shady spot at the south part of town waiting for details to fill canteens at a well near by, an aide-de-camp rode up and said, "General Logan orders this regiment moved immediately outside his lines," and rode away. The regiment did not move with any great degree of alacrity, and was standing to horse, waiting for the canteens to be filled, some twenty minutes later, when the same aide-de-camp dashed up in great wrath and said: "General Logan orders this d—— abolition regiment outside his lines or he will order out a battery and drive it out." The men at once passed along the word and were in the saddle instantly, and the answer came promptly back, "Go and tell Gen. John A. Logan to bring out his battery and we will show him how quick this d—— abolition regiment will take it." The officers tried to move the regiment, but the men sat grim and silent and would not stir. No battery appeared, and finally a compromise was made; the regiment was moved around General Logan's headquarters by a street to the rear, and marched back past his front door with the band playing "John Brown." The command moved out and camped on a stream just south of town, but inside of General Logan's lines.

General Logan was no doubt incensed over Colonel Anthony's order, and other conditions were irritating to him. As soon as the jayhawkers arrived in the South it became the immediate custom for all depredations committed by other troops to be done in their name, and in consequence the Seventh Kansas was compelled to bear opprobrium largely undeserved. The men averaged with the men of other regiments, and were no better or worse as far as honesty went, but at this time they were bearing the aggregated transgressions of regiments from other states. A day or so previous the Second Illinois cavalry had broken into the railway station at Trenton, Tenn., and

had appropriated a considerable quantity of sugar; company A of the Seventh Kansas came up later and also augmented their supply of sweetness. Really not $100 worth of sugar was taken all together, but the owner made a great outcry, and complained through General Logan to General Grant. In September, when the paymaster came to pay the troops, the Seventh Kansas was informed by a messenger from General Grant that if the men would voluntarily consent to the stoppage of two dollars against the pay of each man, to reimburse for this sugar, the men would receive their money; otherwise they would not be paid. It was disrespectful, but word went back by the messenger for "General Grant to go to hell." The stoppage would have amounted to over $1500, and no claim had been made on the Second Illinois cavalry, who were the principal aggressors. The regiment finally received its pay, but it was nearly nine months later when the paymaster made the disbursement.

The First Kansas infantry served with the Seventh in the sixteenth army corps for some time and, of course, sympathized with us, but we never knew how far this sympathy extended until late in the year. While General Grant was making his attempted move toward Vicksburg by way of the Mississippi Central railroad, one morning, as the infantry column was moving south out of Oxford, Miss., the line of march carried it by General Grant's headquarters, and the general himself was sitting on the front veranda smoking and viewing the troops as they passed. Each regiment as it came up was wheeled into line and gave three cheers for the "hero of Donelson." As the First Kansas passed the same program was attempted. The evolution was made all right, but when the cheers were ordered not a sound followed; the men looked up at the sky or away towards the distant landscape, but never at the general, and their lips remained closed. However, as they broke into column and were being led away by their discomfited commander, an old ram in an adjacent corner lot lifted up his voice in a characteristic bleat; the men took it up, and as they marched away down the street plaintive "baas" came back to the ears of the great general.

The regiment arrived at Corinth, Miss., on June 10, and went into camp to the eastward of the town, at Camp Clear Creek. The line of march to camp led by the extensive infantry camps, and the usual interest was manifested. The

jayhawkers were something of a curiosity, and as soon as it became known what this passing cavalry regiment was the road was lined by infantry soldiers. The usual badinage was attempted by the lookers-on, but no response was elicited— the Seventh Kansas rode by with their faces set straight to the front, apparently oblivious to the surroundings; they might have been passing through the desert, as far as any expression of their countenances indicated. The jokes grew fewer and finally ceased entirely, and the infantry men became only silent lookers on. As the rear of the regiment passed one big sergeant said, "I'll be d——." That was the only remark that came to our ears. I mention this, for it was a characteristic of the regiment to ignore surroundings of this nature.

Colonel Lee took command of the regiment on the 17th of July, and on the 20th marched it to Jacinto and from thence to Rienzi, Miss., arriving there on the 23d. Rienzi was the extreme southern outpost of the Northern army. The Seventh Kansas was assigned to the second brigade of the cavalry division; Col. Philip H. Sheridan was our brigade commander; he was at that time a diminutive specimen and did not weigh more than 110 pounds. When he (later) was transferred to the Army of the Cumberland, Colonel Lee became commander of our brigade. Gen. Gordon Granger commanded the cavalry division. The camp of the Seventh Kansas was at this post until its evacuation, September 30. Typhoid fever was prevalent, nineteen deaths resulting in the regiment during a period of about a month. The Confederate army lay about twenty miles to the south, with their advance outposts at Baldwyn and Guntown, and our cavalry was constantly in the saddle. Skirmishes were frequent between opposing scouting parties, and Colonel Lee showed himself to be a dashing and capable cavalry officer. Colonel Sheridan led us on many dashing expeditions, and raids were made into Ripley and through the enemy's lines at Marietta and Bay Springs. At the latter place the Confederate camp was captured and destroyed.

A detachment of the Seventh Kansas had a lively skirmish with a guerrilla leader, who bore the Teutonic name of Funderberger; the affair was always known in the regiment as "the battle of Funderberger's Lane." It was a dashing, picturesque engagement, fought at dusk and after dark, and the

flashing of small arms was exciting and beautiful. It was a running fight, and Funderberger was driven down the lane badly beaten.

On August 26 Faulkner's rebel cavalry drove in our pickets under Captain Eaton, of the Second Iowa cavalry, who were guarding the Ripley road, and charged in nearly to our camp. Most of the command was out on a scout to the south, and matters looked a little dubious for a few minutes. The "sick, lame, and lazy," however, rallied and drove them off. All available men were mounted and started in pursuit; the enemy was routed, and pursued for ten miles. The next day Captain Malone with his company (F) was attacked while scouting on the Kossuth road; he lost four men killed and eight wounded, one of the wounded men dying afterwards. The company rallied and charged the enemy, routing him. Our dead and wounded were recovered, and the Confederates lost three killed. The dead were buried and the wounded brought off the field. About this time Colonel Sheridan received his promotion as brigadier-general and went to Kentucky with Granger's division, and Colonel Lee assumed command of the brigade. Companies B and E took part in the battle of Iuka, fought on the 19th of September, the remainder of the regiment operating on our right flank. General Rosecrans said in his report: "I must not omit to mention the eminent services of Colonel Du Bois, commanding at Rienzi, and Colonel Lee, who, with the Seventh Kansas and part of the Seventh Illinois cavalry, assured our flank and rear during the entire period of our operations." Colonel Lee had not only to guard the flank of Rosecrans's army, but he had to prevent the enemy moving on Corinth, then almost denuded of troops.

After the battle of Iuka the Confederates began to organize for a movement against Corinth. Reenforcements were rushed to them, and the 1st of October their advance began. The Seventh Kansas operated on their right flank and harassed the movements of the Confederates, participating in several sharp skirmishes. On the night of October 3 the regiment entered Corinth by the Kossuth road in time to take part in the terrible battle of the next day. When the regiment entered, it was supposed the Kossuth road lay a half mile to the right of the Confederate flank. Lovell, who commanded their right, had, after dark however, extended his lines across the road, it being the Confederate plan to open the battle in

-3

the morning by an attack by Lovell on College hill. He did not want to expose the new disposition of his troops, so let us pass through his lines, expecting to have us the next day anyhow. It was a bright moonlight night, and the way appeared innocent enough, but Lovell could have swept us out of existence any moment with the artillery and musketry masked in the brush along our line of march. I have often wondered if the Confederate Colonel Jackson, whose cavalry division, formed on the right, was guarding this road, ever knew that the regiment he permitted to pass by in safety was the same that less than two months later assaulted and decisively whipped his whole division in the Lamar lane. The Seventh Kansas operated mostly on our left flank, and were deployed in the abattis as sharpshooters. The regiment was conspicuous in the pursuit, until it ended at Ripley; it took part in many sharp skirmishes, repeatedly defeating Baxter's rebel cavalry brigade and capturing many prisoners.

The night we entered Ripley, during the pursuit, Captain Houston, with company H, was stationed as picket on the road leading south from town. Suspecting a move on the part of the enemy, he caused a fire to be built, and arranged dummies in imitation of soldiers lying asleep about the smoldering embers, and then posted his company in the brush down the road. Sure enough, about two o'clock in the morning a Confederate company came stealing up the road and, deploying, moved silently on their supposed sleeping victims. Houston noiselessly deployed his company in their rear and stealthily followed. At the proper distance the Confederates drew a bead on the dummies, and the captain exultingly demanded a surrender. "Had you not better surrender yourself?" said Captain Houston, quietly. The startled Confederates turned and discovered a line of Yankee carbines, with a man behind each one, drawn level at their heads. They promptly obeyed Captain Houston's injunction and surrendered. It was a neat job and resulted in over forty prisoners, including several officers.

Referring to prisoners, I wish to record here that the entire number of the Seventh Kansas made prisoners of war during over four years of active service would not aggregate a score, and in but one instance was ever more than one taken at one time. The exception was Lieutenant Osgood, and, I believe, two men, picked up near Rienzi, Miss., in the fall of 1862.

Several times were squads and companies nearly surrounded by superior numbers, but they fought their way out and made their escape.

The battle of Corinth is a matter of history and students of the civil war know how severe the fighting was. Our forces numbered about 20,000 and the Confederates about 40,000. We, of course, had the advantage of position and the chain of redoubts that strengthened our line. The writer was an orderly at General Rosecrans's headquarters during the last day of the engagement, and was privileged in seeing more of a severe battle than usually falls to the lot of one individual. Orders went out thick and fast and staff officers and orderlies rode the lines with rapid frequency. When the victory was achieved, I had the privilege of riding in the train of the great general when he rode along the lines and thanked his regiments for the victory they had given him. The Confederate dead still lay along our front, and, especially in front of Fort Robinet, the slaughter had been fearful.

On its return from the pursuit the regiment went into camp for a few days east of Corinth, on the Farmington road. From this point a raid was made across Bear creek into Alabama, as far as Buzzard Roost station. Roddy's command was met and driven back, badly whipped. A most gallant act was performed here by Sergt. Alonzo Dickson and three men of company H, who led the advance. As they came in sight of the Confederate outpost, although it consisted of about fifteen men, they at once dashed forward, and the rebels mounted their horses and fled in a panic. Dickson and his squad pursued them over a mile, killing over half of their number and capturing several; but two or three escaped.

On the return of the regiment from this expedition, it received orders to move to Grand Junction, where General Grant was concentrating an army for a movement against Vicksburg. The Confederate army, under General Pemberton, was encamped along the Coldwater, about twenty miles to the south. On November 8 a reconnoisance in force was made under the command of General McPherson towards Hudsonville. The Seventh Kansas led the advance on the main road and moved about two miles ahead of the infantry column. Near Lamar it came on the flank of the Confederate cavalry division under the command of Colonel Jackson, General Pemberton's chief of cavalry. Captain Gregory, who held our ad-

vance with his company (E), immediately attacked, and was followed by an assault by the whole regiment. The Confederates were completely routed, and fled, leaving their dead and wounded and many prisoners in our hands. They left thirty-six dead and 400 or 500 prisoners, many severely wounded, and nearly 2000 stand of arms. The glory of this victory will appear more pronounced when it is understood that the attack was made by one small regiment, numbering about 600 men, nearly two miles away from any support, and against a division numbering 4000. This defeat caused the retreat of the entire Confederate army to a point below Holly Springs, and the victory gave Colonel Lee his star. The regiment advanced the same evening to the enemy's lines and drew his artillery fire, but his cavalry were too badly demoralized to offer any opposition. On the return to the camp at Grand Junction the regiment was received by the infantry with cheers.

November 27, 1862, the advance of the army began. The Seventh Kansas led the advance of the main infantry column, and on the morning of the 28th charged into Holly Springs, capturing the pickets on the Hudsonville road, routing the garrison, and driving the Confederates beyond the town. The regiment was given the post of honor and held the extreme advance most of the time during the forward movement, fighting almost constantly from dawn until well into the night, and then finding rest disturbed by the playful shells which the enemy would explode over its exposed bivouac. The Confederates contested every foot of the way between Holly Springs and the Tallahatchie with cavalry and artillery, but the Seventh Kansas steadily pushed them back. Ten miles below Holly Springs a Confederate force supporting a twelve-pound gun was charged and the gun captured. The enemy finally retired within their fortifications that stretched along the Tallahatchie river, and as the jayhawkers came within range of their big guns proceeded to give them the benefit of the concentrated fire of some forty siege pieces. Half an hour later, when the infantry supports came up, the First Kansas infantry led the advance. They came on at the double-quick, and as they piled their blankets and knapsacks and deployed in the field beyond our left each company would give hearty cheers for the jayhawkers and the jayhawkers returned them as heartily, telling them to "Give 'em Wilson Creek." Shells

were bursting overhead or ricochetting across the fields, and the Seventh was much relieved when the infantry came up; and it was especially pleasing to have this splendid fighting regiment from our home state come to our support. Several times during this advance would we see an infantry regiment away across the fields tossing their caps in the air and cheering; we knew that it was the First Kansas, who by some infallible means always recognized their brothers from home and sent them greeting.

At nightfall the infantry fell back out of range, and left the Seventh to picket the advance line. During the night scouts were sent forward; Sergeant Henry, of company D, with two men, crept within the forts on the left of the road, and confirmed the suspicion that the Confederates were evacuating. Sergeant Wildey and one man of company C crawled through their pickets and across a cotton field on the right to the vicinity of the bridge, and returned with a confirmation of the report. At daylight the Seventh Kansas advanced and found the earthworks dismantled, the enemy in full retreat, and the bridge over the Tallahatchie destroyed. Again the jayhawkers led the advance on the main road. It had rained heavily during the night and the roads were very muddy, but that did not delay to any great extent. The enemy's rear guard was struck soon, but was easily pushed back until within a mile of Oxford, where they were reenforced, and a strong stand was made, supported by one piece of artillery. They opened at short range with double-shotted canister, and did considerable damage to the oak undergrowth. Lieut. James Smith led company C in a charge directly against the artillery, but they were handling the gun by fixed prolonge and succeeded in dragging it out of reach. At the edge of town the entire regiment dismounted and deployed for the final rush; first, however, Captain Swoyer led company B in a mounted charge in column down the main street, but, meeting a heavy fire from the public square, was forced to retire. When the formation was complete the order to advance was given, and the men went in with a yell. Strong opposition was met, especially at the court-house square, but this force, seeing that they would be flanked, fell back with the rest, leaving a number of dead and prisoners in our hands. During the fight a man was noticed standing on the observatory of a large house watching our advance through a field-glass. A bullet fired at him struck

the railing near by. He disappeared, and in a few minutes was seen galloping away to a place of safety. That man was the Hon. Jacob Thompson, formerly secretary of the interior under President Buchanan.

The next day the regiment pushed forward as far as Water Valley, skirmishing the entire distance and capturing nearly a thousand prisoners, who were straggling behind the retreating army. Late in the afternoon a captured drummer boy was trudging back along our column to take his place with the other prisoners: "Where are you going, Johnny?" was asked him; "Back to the rear to beat roll-call for Pemberton's army," was his prompt answer. That evening, as the regiment was formed in a hollow square around the prisoners, our boys, who had supplied themselves with a bountiful store of tobacco at the expense of the Oxford merchants, discovered that the prisoners were destitute and fainting for a "chaw of stingy green," and so began to pitch whole plugs of "flat," which was a luxury, to the suffering Johnnies. It created a transformation; despondency disappeared and contentment took its place; three cheers for the jayhawkers were given with a gusto, and the little drummer boy of the afternoon came forward and regaled the regiment with the rebel version of the "Happy Land of Canaan," a song much in vogue during the first years of the war. One verse still clings to my memory:

> "Old John Brown came to Harper's Ferry town,
>   Old John Brown was a game one;
>   But we led him up a slope, and we let him down a rope,
>   And sent him to the happy land of Canaan."

That night the regiment picketed the main road at the burning bridge across the Otuckalofa. Fording the river early in the morning the pursuit was continued, the Seventh Kansas still leading the advance. Sharp skirmishing continued during the day until after noon, when the resistance grew lighter. The cavalry had pressed forward nearly thirty miles in advance of the infantry supports, and the enemy, cognizant of this, had prepared a surprise. About a mile north of Coffeyville, Lovell's infantry division had been posted in the timber with two six-gun batteries masked in the brush, and a large cavalry force on each flank. Companies A, G, I and K deployed as skirmishers, were advancing dismounted across an open field when they were received by a withering volley from

the rebel infantry and artillery. These companies fell back to the belt of timber in the rear, and rallied on company C coming forward in support; the five companies then fell slowly back, contesting the Confederate advance every inch of the way across a field to the rear until our main line, which was rapidly forming along the edge of the timber on the next slope, was reached. The Confederates numbered from 8000 to 10,-000, supported by two batteries, while the Union forces were scarcely 4000 dismounted cavalry, with but two twelve-pound guns, and entirely without reserves; yet our position was maintained for over half an hour, and until the Confederate force had swung around our flanks and had us nearly surrounded. Our loss was heavy but that of the Southerners very much greater. The Seventh Kansas, with detachments of other regiments, made a fine stand at a bridge across a deep stream to the rear and repulsed the final charge of the rebels. The entire command fell back to Water Valley.

The battle of Coffeyville was fought on December 5, 1862. Our regimental loss was eight killed and about forty wounded. Lieut. Tom Woodburn, a gallant officer, fell at the head of his company; Lieutenant Colbert was wounded, and Colonel Lee's horse was wounded beneath him. We lost no prisoners. Our artillery, supported by the Seventh Kansas, was served until the charging Confederates were within a hundred feet of the muzzles and then was successfully dragged away at fixed prolonge, with a sergeant riding the last gun, facing to the rear with his thumb to his nose at the eluded rebels, who sent a shower of bullets after him.

The report of the Confederate general says: "The tactics of the enemy did them great credit." Among our dead was Private Francis Schilling, a German of fine education and great refinement. He came to Kansas from Chicago and joined the Seventh Kansas, led hither by his extreme abolition belief. He was a frequent correspondent of the Chicago *Tribune*. He fell with his face to the foe, dying for a principle, if ever a man did during the history of this world.

The cavalry division fell back to the Yocknapatalfa and encamped at Prophet bridge. From this point company A scouted back to the vicinity of the Coffeyville battle-field and secured information of the raid against our line of communication, just starting under the leadership of the rebel general, Van Dorn. Securing complete details of the movement, the

company returned rapidly and reported to Colonel Dickey. He received the report with incredulity and neglected to report to General Grant until eight hours later. When General Grant finally received the information he instantly ordered all the cavalry by forced marches to Holly Springs. The Seventh Kansas moved out in advance and rode the forty miles with scarcely a halt, and with jaded horses reached Holly Springs at about ten o'clock the next morning, in advance of all the rest, but about an hour after the rebels had destroyed the vast amount of supplies stored there and had moved north. The delay of Colonel Dickey had been fatal. Had he sent the information forward without delay, reenforcements would have easily reached Holly Srings in time to have beaten off Van Dorn and saved the town, with millions of dollars' worth of stores. The regiment immediately pushed north to Bolivar, Van Dorn's next objective point, reaching there in advance of the rebel raider. The garrison was small, but a determined show of force was made, and Van Dorn feared to attack, and immediately began a hasty retreat. The Seventh Kansas followed, constantly skirmishing with him until he passed south of Pontotoc.

The regiment returned to Holly Springs, and on the 31st of December moved north to Moscow, Tenn., and later to Germantown, where the command wintered. The march north was in the wake of our retiring army; buildings and fences were burning, and frequent detours had to be made to pass places too hot for comfort or safety of ammunition. I wish some of our ultra sentimentalists who are posing at the present day, and whose souls are full of metaphorical tears for the cruel acts of the American army, could have seen some of the gentle touches of the civil war. But most of these gentlemen, if of a suitable age, took extreme care to be absent from the scenes of ignoble strife.

At Germantown Colonel Lee[5] received notice of his promo-

5. BRIGADIER GENERAL ALBERT LINDLEY LEE died at the Hotel Belmont, New York, December 31, 1907, of pleurisy. He was born in Fulton, Oswego county, New York, January 16, 1834. He graduated from Union College in 1853. He practiced law in New York city from 1855 to 1857. In 1857 he moved to Kansas. In 1859 he was in the newspaper business with D. W. Wilder at Elwood, Doniphan county. In that year he was defeated as a candidate to the Wyandotte constitutional convention. In the fall he was elected judge of the district court, under the Wyandotte constitution, for the counties of Atchison, Brown, Marshall, Nemaha and Doniphan, over George W. Glick. The state was not admitted until January 29, 1861, and he served only six months as judge, enlisting in October. He was voted for as a candidate for Congress in 1864 against Sidney Clarke. He returned to the state in August, 1866, and in 1867 he received twenty-five votes for United States senator. He was in New Orleans as a newspaper editor for some time, and about 1890 went to New York and became a banker and broker.

tion as brigadier-general, and took leave of the regiment. He was a fine officer, brave, dashing, and ambitious. General Grant commended him highly, and placed him in command of the brigade when General Sheridan was transferred to Kentucky. In a dispatch to General Halleck, dated November 11, 1862, General Grant said: "Colonel Lee is one of our best cavalry officers; I earnestly recommend him for promotion." Lieutenant-colonel Herrick continued in command of the regiment after Colonel Lee's promotion. While stationed at Germantown the regiment was almost constantly in the saddle, patrolling the roads and scouting far out into the country. A number of sharp skirmishes were fought, with unvarying success to our side.

On the 15th of April, 1863, the Seventh Kansas moved to Corinth, Miss., arriving there on the 17th, and the next morning marched to join General Dodge, who was concentrating a considerable force at Bear creek, preparatory to a movement into Alabama. The army crossed Bear creek on the 24th. At Tuscumbia the regiment attacked the rebels under General Roddy and drove them out of the town, carrying the place by a brilliant charge. The capture of Tuscumbia was followed by the immediate advance of the cavalry brigade, under command of Colonel Cornyn, of the Tenth Missouri cavalry, an impetuous leader, who hated a rebel as he did the devil. The enemy was met a short distance out. He opened up on the Seventh Kansas, leading the advance, with artillery, but was soon driven back to within a mile of Leighton, where he made a determined stand with artillery strongly posted on an elevation to the left of the road. The Seventh held the left of the line and advanced against this position. The Tenth Missouri held the road with a mounted battalion, with the rest of the regiment deployed dismounted in the field on the right. A light mountain battery of five guns, supported by a battalion of the Seventh Kansas, was advanced close under the muzzles of the heavy cannon of the enemy and fairly smothered them with their rapid fire. Captain Utt at the same time led a charge of three companies around the left against their battery. Companies B and H judiciously swerved to the left and opened fire with their small arms from the shelter of the timber, but Captain Utt led company A square in the face of the artillery. It was another case of the sunken road of Ohain; an impassable fence intervened—one of those straight fences

bound together with hickory withes. Captain Utt's leg was carried away and his horse killed beneath him by a charge of grape. The company was compelled to retreat.

The whole command then assaulted and the rebels were driven back two miles beyond Leighton. Colonel Cornyn withdrew his cavalry at nightfall to Tuscumbia, where he lay until the morning of the 27th. This engagement was fought against a superior force, but the result was a splendid victory. General Dodge in his official report says, relative to this battle: "The command consisted on our part of the Tenth Missouri and Seventh Kansas cavalry, about 800 in all, driving the enemy eight miles. The enemy's force was 3500, besides one battery. The fighting of the cavalry against such odds is beyond all praise."

A second advance was made on the 27th, led by Cornyn's brigade. The enemy was met in force and driven beyond Town creek. At that stream a severe engagement took place. The infantry supports came up and a heavy artillery duel, which lasted several hours, occurred. From Town creek the entire infantry command fell back to Corinth. The cavalry fell back to Burnsville, Miss., and then moved rapidly to the south. This last movement was in conjunction with the advance of General Grierson, just ready to start on his great raid through Mississippi. Cornyn's brigade moved on the left and in advance of Grierson. The enemy were soon met, and constant skirmishing was kept up until the command reached Tupelo.

At this place, on May 5, was met a strong force under the command of the rebel Generals Gholson and Ruggles. The rebels were preparing an elaborate plan to capture our whole command, and they had the force to do it, but Cornyn did not do his part to make it a success. Instead of deploying at the bridge and being two or three hours forcing a crossing, the Seventh Kansas charged it in column, was over it in five minutes, and the enemy were caught with their forces divided. Company A of the Seventh came suddenly on the flank of a rebel cavalry regiment moving down under the shelter of some tenant Sanders attacked at once, and the surprised Confederates were driven down on the Tenth Missouri, who charged, and the entire rebel regiment was captured. A number were killed and wounded, and many of the prisoners bore marks of the saber that played a conspicuous part in this division of the

fight. Company A lost but one man killed, Corp. Edwin M. Vaughn. While this fighting was going on General Gholson, supposing their plan was meeting with success, came up through the timber on the left with his infantry, to catch our column on the flank and rear and complete the conquest. He ran into the Tenth Missouri's mountain battery, supported by companies I and K of the Seventh Kansas, and met a galling fire of double-shotted canister and rapid volleys from the supporting companies. Company C charged in on his right flank and poured volley after volley into his charging lines. Gholson's infantry were largely raw levies and could not stand the cross-fire they were subjected to; they wavered, then turned and fled, in a panic. The timber was strewn with corn bread and haversacks as far as our pursuit extended. They did not attempt to follow when, at night, according to plan, Cornyn fell back, nor did they molest Grierson's column as he passed. The loss of the enemy was heavy in killed and wounded, and the prisoners numbered several hundred, including a large number of officers.

The regiment had permanent headquarters at Corinth after its return until January 8, 1864. The duties performed during the summer and fall of 1863 were arduous—scouting and skirmishing daily, and keeping a constant surveillance over the movements of the enemy. Many severe engagements with Forrest were fought, and the work was always well and bravely done. Until the fall of Vicksburg, constant watch was maintained to prevent reenforcements going to Johnston. On July 11, 1863, Lieutenant-colonel Herrick was promoted to colonel, and Captain Houston, of company H, lieutenant-colonel.

On the 26th of May, 1863, Colonel Cornyn, with a mounted force consisting of the Seventh Kansas, Tenth Missouri, and one battalion of the Fifteenth Illinois cavalry, and the Ninth Illinois mounted infantry, moved towards the Tennessee river. The river was crossed at Hamburg during the night, and the whole force advanced towards Florence, Ala., the Seventh Kansas leading the advance. During the day two companies of the regiment made a detour to Rawhide, out on the left flank, and destroyed the large grist-mill and the cotton and woolen factories located there and employed in manufacturing material for the enemy. The Confederate cavalry were met about ten miles out of Florence. They contested our advance,

but were easily forced back. Their pickets were driven in, but the forces composing the garrison of the place were found posted along the west edge of town, supported by artillery. Their cannon were quickly silenced and the place carried by assault, and their entire force, which was commanded by General Villepigue, driven beyond the town. A large quantity of fixed ammunition and a number of shops making war material were destroyed, and seven large cotton and woolen factories were burned; also large quantities of corn and forage belonging to the Confederate government. As the command moved out to the southward after nightfall it was attacked, and a severe encounter took place. The enemy was driven off but returned to the attack repeatedly, and more or less skirmishing lasted during the night. A major and about fifty men were captured by a charge of a company of the regiment; after that the enemy became more cautious. The Seventh Kansas covered the rear while the brigade was crossing the river on the return, and repulsed several sharp attacks, and, finally, making a countercharge, drove the enemy back over a mile. The brigade returned to Corinth on the 29th. During this raid the Seventh Kansas was in the saddle constantly during five days and four nights, never resting more than two hours at any one time.

Col. Florence M. Cornyn, of the Tenth Missouri cavalry, who commanded our brigade for several months, was a redheaded Irishman, absolutely fearless, of iron constitution. and untiring while in the field. He never stopped to ascertain the number of the enemy's force, but attacked at once wherever he was met. His audacity always won out and never failed to score a victory. He was shot and killed by his lieutenant-colonel in a personal encounter in the fall of 1863. The raids that we made under him were dashing and always produced great results, and it used to be said in discussing the forays that he led, that "Solomon in all his glory was not arrayed like one of these."

It will be too long a story to go into detail in describing·all the engagements which the regiment participated in during the season of 1863. It was a year of constant work and weary night marches, through mud and rain or stifling dust, and many sharp encounters occurred with Forrest.

It will be remembered that the year 1863—the turning-point in the war—was a season of great activity. In northern

Mississippi Forrest was operating to keep reenforcements from Grant and Rosecrans, and the Union forces, which were really the outposts of Grant's army operating before Vicksburg until after Pemberton's surrender, were constantly employed in scouting and watching to prevent reenforcements going to Johnston. Forrest was the most skilful of all the Confederate cavalry generals. He was almost ubiquitous, constantly on the move, and, operating as he did in a country friendly to the cause of the South, gave us no end of work. Forrest never seemed to think the life of a man of much consequence when he had a purpose to accomplish. He exposed his men recklessly and suffered heavy losses, but at the same time forced the Union cavalry frequently to take desperate chances to offset his movements. In telling the story of 1863, one can give but little idea of the constant strain the little force in northern Mississippi was subjected to. The Seventh Kansas, nominally in camp at Corinth, spent very little time there; the raids into the Tuscumbia valley, to Tupelo, and across the Tennessee river to Florence, already briefly described, are but samples of the work performed until the regiment was veteranized and went north on furlough. After the fall of Vicksburg, every effort was made to hold Forrest with as large a Confederate force as possible in Mississippi and prevent his reenforcing Bragg. Movements to the north and east as well as to the east and south were made, and numerous affairs that entailed more hardship than loss of life resulted from frequent contact with the enemy, and many small encounters of. more significance than appeared on the surface will be passed over in this story, in which only the most conspicuous affairs are described.

On March 12, 1863, a fight with Richardson near Gallaway station, Tenn., ended in a rout of the enemy. Colonel Looney, Major Sanford and Captain Bright, of the Confederate army, were captured, together with a considerable number of enlisted men.

On March 16, near Mount Pleasant, Miss., the Confederates were whipped and their rear-guard captured.

On April 2-6 a series of sharp engagements occurred, which resulted in the defeat of the enemy.

On September 30 companies A and C attacked the rear-guard of a Confederate force crossing the Tennessee river at Swallow Bluffs, Tenn. The rear-guard of the enemy, con-

sisting of a major and thirty men, was captured. The fighting was severe. Our loss was one man killed and five wounded. The enemy lost several killed.

On October 12 and 13 the regiment participated in a sharp battle with Forrest at Byhalia and Wyatt. The Seventh Kansas made a number of brilliant charges, and Forrest was eventually driven across the Tallahatchie with heavy loss in killed and wounded. In this engagement Capt. Amos Hodgeman was mortally wounded, while leading a charge against the enemy. He died on the 16th. The fighting lasted three days, beginning at Quinn's mill, south of Colliersville, and ending with the severe cavalry battle at Wyatt, on the 13th. A number of prisoners, including several prominent officers, were captured.

The cavalry engagement at Wyatt was an affair of considerable magnitude, and during the first year of the civil war would have easily ranked as a battle. Sharp fighting began about three o'clock in the afternoon, and lasted with little intermission until ten at night. Our force consisted of the Seventh Kansas cavalry, the Third, Sixth and Seventh Illinois cavalry, Ninth Illinois mounted infantry, Third Michigan and Sixth Tennessee cavalry, and eight pieces of artillery. The rebel force was a cavalry division numbering about 6000, reenforced with artillery. A severe thunder-storm, with heavy downpour of rain, lasted during the whole time. Our last charge was made by Phillips's brigade, consisting of the Seventh Kansas, Third Michigan and Sixth Tennessee cavalry, and Phillips's own gallant regiment, the Ninth Illinois mounted infantry. The troops were dismounted, and the charge was made at nine o'clock, in pitch darkness, and the enemy's position indicated only by the flashing of small arms and artillery. Over fences, across ditches, and through mud, our men went up and carried the enemy's position, driving him across the Tallahatchie river, and, following close on his heels, prevented the destruction of the bridge, which he attempted.

That grim sense of humor that can see a joke in the face of death found an opportunity for exercise just before this charge began. Major Malone, who was mounted, rode out in front of the regiment, preparing to lead the coming charge, with the remark that "we'll drive 'em to hell!" and then vanished from sight. A smothered and distant voice from the bowels of the earth at last indicated his whereabouts. Halter-

straps were spliced and let down, and he was dragged up, considerably jarred, but not otherwise injured. A measurement was made the next morning from the surface to the saddle on the dead horse; the distance was thirty-two feet. The well was dry and not walled, and the caving earth probably broke the fall and saved the life of the major. When we asked him what he thought as he was going down, he said: "Thought? I thought that I was going to hell on horseback."

On December 1 the regiment was engaged at Ripley, with a superior command led by General Forrest in person. The Seventh Kansas had been sent to retard the advance of the rebels on the Memphis & Charleston railroad. The action was severe and full of hardship and danger, but the Confederates were held back and the jayhawkers came off with honor. Maj. W. S. Jenkins was severely wounded in the head in this engagement.

On December 24 a battalion of the regiment defeated a detachment of Forrest's command at Jack's Creek, Tenn.

On the 1st day of January, 1864, while the Seventh Kansas lay in temporary camp below Wolf river, south of La Grange, Tenn., the subject of reenlisting as veterans was taken up. The men were bivouacked in the snow, without shelter, and the weather was bitter cold; they were returning from a raid into Mississippi, and the last two days' march had been made through rain, sleet, and snow. Before night over four-fifths of the regiment had signed the reenlistment papers and stood ready for "three years more." The Seventh Kansas was the first regiment to reenlist in that part of the army, and was the only Kansas organization to enlist as a regiment and maintain, as veterans, the full regimental organization. The regiment at once moved to Corinth. On January 18 camp was broken and the command proceeded to Memphis, where, on January 21, the veterans were mustered, to date from the 1st of January, 1864. The men who did not reenlist immediately became known as the "bobtails." They looked sad as the regiment went aboard the transports to go north to their homes for a month's furlough, and a number, who could stand it no longer, reenlisted at the last moment. The "bobtails" were assigned to other regiments and remained in the field and continued to do excellent service. They joined the regiment again on its return south in June, and served with it until their discharge.

At Cairo the veterans were paid, and then proceeded towards Kansas by way of Decatur and Quincy, Ill., and St. Joseph, Mo.; the objective point was Fort Leavenworth. The men enjoyed themselves on the journey, and made no end of fun. At Decatur, Ill., the men discovered that the landlord of the eating station was charging them seventy-five cents for dinner, while he was charging civilians but fifty. The landlord was up against trouble at once, and, realizing it, fled from danger and hid in the attic. He was soon found and dragged out, and, begging for mercy, promised restitution. Probably not more than a hundred of the men had eaten at his hotel, but the whole regiment suddenly assembled and fell in, and, when payment began, as soon as the man on the right received his twenty-five-cent shinplaster he would drop out and fall in again on the left. Had not the train for Quincy pulled out soon that hotel-keeper must have been a bankrupt. At Weston, Mo., the ferryman refused to cross the regiment to the Kansas side at the expense of the government, because he had had difficulty in collecting pay for similar service. The captain of the boat was promptly set on shore, Lieut. D. C. Taylor took the wheel, while several men manned the engines below. As soon as loaded, the boat swung out, made the crossing, and never knew that it had changed crews.

At the landing above Fort Leavenworth the regiment was met by a delegation of Leavenworth citizens and received with honors. The men were accorded the freedom of the city; formal action in this direction was unnecessary, for the boys would have taken it anyhow.

At the end of their furloughs the men assembled at Fort Leavenworth and again were paid off, and March 12, 1864, sailed towards Memphis. At St. Louis, however, the regiment was halted, and went ashore and remained there in camp on the old Camp Gamble grounds until June 6. Having been reequipped, it moved by river transports to Memphis, Tenn. On the 17th of June the Seventh Kansas left Memphis and moved out along the Memphis & Charleston railroad, to cover the retreat of a portion of Sturgis's command, defeated at Guntown, Miss., by General Forrest.*

---

6. There is a story I would be glad to write, if I can get sufficient data, of another company K boy, Arthur T. Reeve. He was hospital steward of the Seventh Kansas, promoted captain of company D, Forty-fifth U. S. colored infantry. It is the story of his heroism in bringing his company off the field when General Sturges was defeated by General Forrest at Guntown, Miss. He marched his company over 150 miles through the enemy's country, fighting almost every foot of the entire way.

On July 5, the regiment moved from La Grange, Tenn., as the advance-guard of Gen. A. J. Smith's infantry column, starting south on its expedition against General Forrest. General Smith had detached the Seventh Kansas from Grierson's cavalry division and given them the post of honor with the main column, which it retained until Pontotoc was reached and captured, and then on the never-to-be-forgotten 13th of July was trusted to cover the rear-guard during the movement from Pontotoc to Tupelo. The advance from the beginning was opposed by the enemy in considerable force, but the Seventh Kansas kept the main road clear, and the march of the infantry column was never retarded; the remaining cavalry force operated on the flanks.

On the 10th a sharp fight was had with Barteau's cavalry, and they were badly whipped and driven back, with the loss of five men killed and left on the field. Approaching Pontotoc on the 11th, the enemy was met in force, and a sharp engagement followed. He was driven back on Pontotoc with heavy loss, but General McCulloch, with a brigade of rebel cavalry, held the town. The Seventh Kansas was reenforced by a brigade of infantry and drove in the rebel skirmishers. Grierson's cavalry attacked at the same time from the east. The Confederates were driven from their position and retreated in disorder, leaving their dead and wounded in our hands. The main force of the enemy was fortified on Cherry creek, about eight miles south of Pontotoc. General Smith rested on the 12th, and gave General Forrest an opportunity to come out and attack, which he failed to take advantage of. Early on the morning of the 13th Grierson's cavalry was pushed rapidly to the east, with instruction to seize a position at Tupelo, about eighteen miles distant. The infantry, followed by the train, pushed out immediately after, leaving the Seventh Kansas drawn up in line of battle waiting for the Confederate advance. The attack came soon after daylight, and the regiment slowly fell back, contesting every inch of the way. For-

As I recall it, his other officers were not with him. It was a heroic piece of work that stands alone for steady, persistent nerve. If they had surrendered they would have been murdered to a man, so they fought their way through for days without rest or sleep. Major Reeve settled in Iowa after the war. Nearly twenty years ago he promised to give me his detailed story of his retreat, but he died soon after, and I never heard his statement. The Seventh Kansas returned from veteran furlough while Sturges was on this expedition, and the news of his disaster met us at Memphis as we landed. We were pushed out hurriedly to help cover his retreat, and were fortunate enough to be the ones who met Captain Reeve with the remnant of his company below La Grange.

—4

rest had thrown his infantry forward to the east, on a parallel road to Pontotoc, and sent his cavalry to our rear to pursue. Twice during the day he attacked in force from the right, but was repulsed by the Minnesota brigade guarding that flank of the train.

To the Seventh Kansas, under the command of Colonel Herrick, had been assigned the duty of guarding the rear of the train against a division of cavalry. It was done, but how it was done is difficult to understand; it was the accomplishment of a seeming impossibility. Every point of advantage was seized and held to the last moment. Squadrons were detached and fought in isolated positions on the flanks, to give impression of a stronger force. Early in the day company A was dismounted and placed in ambush, at the risk of probable capture. They caught the Confederate advance coming on too confidently and emptied many saddles, sending their advance regiment back in confusion. Company A regained their horses in safety, and this deed had a restraining influence on the Confederate cavalry during the rest of the day. The enemy immediately brought up artillery and shelled the timber in advance, as a precaution against similar attempts. Company C fought once on the left in an isolated position until nearly surrounded, and then cut their way out and escaped. The Confederate advance was made in three columns; if you checked one the others came on and threatened your flank. The Seventh Kansas covered the rear alone during the whole forenoon; later, Colonel Bouton, commanding a colored brigade, dropped back to its support. During the day three distinct charges were made on the rear of the column, which were handsomely repulsed by the Seventh and Bouton's brigade. Forrest says in his report, relative to the conduct of the Seventh Kansas that day, "He took advantage of every favorable position, and my artillery was kept almost constantly busy."

This tells but little of the constant fighting done by the jayhawkers from five in the morning until nine in the evening, when they passed to the rear of the infantry line of battle, formed to meet the attacks of the following day. Supperless the men dropped to sleep, and lay as dead until the enemy's shells bursting overhead in the early morning caused them to turn, and at last one by one to raise up and utter maledictions at the "man that shot the gun." This day's work was one of

the best that the regiment ever did, and Colonel Herrick showed how much genuine stuff there was in him during the trying time when desperate fighting and skilful maneuvering were necessary to hold a much superior force in check.

The Seventh Kansas with a portion of the cavalry division guarded the right of the line during the battle and was but lightly engaged. The battle of Tupelo was a bloody engagement, and the Confederates suffered terrible losses; some regiments were wiped out of existence.

At noon on the 15th General Smith began to move north by the Ellistown road, the Seventh Kansas taking the advance and skirmishing constantly, until camp at Town creek was reached. On the day following the regiment took the rear, and contended all day with McCulloch's Confederate brigade until Ellistown was approached; here a sharp, almost hand-to-hand engagement was fought, which resulted to the discomfiture of the enemy.

During the afternoon Major Gregory, who had been sent back on an intersecting road with two companies to guard against an attack on our flank, had remained too long, and, as he finally came down through the timber that lined the road to join the main column, discovered that the head of the Confederate cavalry advance was passing the intersection of the roads and was pushing on rapidly after the rear of our regiment. Gregory had not been seen, and could have easily withdrawn his command and, by making a detour, regained the regiment, but that was not his manner of doing things. He instantly ordered his men to draw pistol and charge by file down upon and along the flank of the enemy. The movement was brilliantly executed; the Confederate cavalry was taken absolutely by surprise, and our men rode by, Gregory bringing up the rear, emptying their revolvers into the rebel flank without a shot being returned. Many saddles must have been emptied, but our men were not waiting to count dead Johnnies. With a parting shot they galloped across an intervening ford and rejoined the main column without the loss of a man.

From Ellistown the march was unmolested, and the regiment arrived at La Grange on the 19th of July, 1864.

On August 9 General Smith again moved from La Grange to Oxford, Miss. The Seventh Kansas, assigned to Hatch's division, moved on the 1st to Holly Springs. On the 8th a severe engagement was fought at Tallahatchie river, in which

the regiment was engaged. The enemy was whipped and driven across the river in retreat. On the 9th heavy skirmishing continued eight miles to Hurricane creek, where the enemy was found in force occupying the heights on the opposite side. He was driven back with loss and his strong position carried. The pursuit continued to Oxford. At this point the enemy made a stand, supported by artillery; he was again driven back, with the loss of his caissons and camp equipage. Our cavalry force then fell back to Abbeville. During this expedition a considerable portion of Oxford was burned by our troops. Much censure was heaped on General Smith's command for this act of vandalism. I wish to state here that the day this was done Southern newspapers fell into our hands glorying over the burning of Chambersburg, Pa. This was the first news that we had received of this act of incendiarism, and Oxford was burned in retaliation.

On the 13th a second advance was made, and Forrest was again found occupying his former strong position on the opposite side of Hurricane creek. The Seventh Kansas was a part of Herrick's brigade, which composed the left wing. The enemy's right was assaulted and driven back across the stream. In the meantime heavy fighting was going on at the left and center, where the enemy was badly beaten and forced to retire. This defeat caused him to withdraw his right, and Herrick advanced and occupied his position. The enemy retreated rapidly on Oxford and the Union forces were again withdrawn to the Tallahatchie. This last battle at Hurricane creek was an affair of considerable magnitude; it was purely a cavalry battle, no infantry being engaged.

Grim-visaged war, if not always able to smooth his wrinkled front, must even in times of stress sometimes let a crease or two slip down to the corners of his mouth, to create the semblance of a smile; otherwise the monotony of solemn things would become too serious to be borne. A smile may be permitted here, after twoscore years, and all about a pair of trousers.

Just as this expedition moved from La Grange in the lightest of marching order, Captain Thornton appeared arrayed in a pair of buckskin breeches; "Not regulation," he said, "but durable." We had all recently returned from a similar expedition with trousers showing many a gaping rift, created by the constant friction of the saddle, and he would not be caught

that way again, he said, not he. The day before the cavalry fight at Hurricane creek it rained, and we were in the saddle during the downpour and thoroughly wet through, and Thornton's buckskin breeches, soaked and soggy, became a sort of tenacious pulp. That night he improvised a clothes-line and hung them out to dry. At early reveille he sought his trousers; they were there. But you know what can be done with wet buckskin! Some evil-disposed person, under the cover of the night, had stretched them until they looked like a pair of gigantic tongs—they were twenty feet long if they were an inch. The cavalry battle of Hurricane creek was fought that day, and Thornton led his company, but it was in a costume that must have made pleasant to him the knowledge that the exigencies of war debarred the presence of the female sex. There was a hiatus between the extremity of the undergarment that obtruded below his cavalry jacket and his boots. Thornton was a Scotchman, and we accused him of coming out in kilts. He turned his trousers over to his colored servant in the early morning, and the faithful darky rode that day in the wake of battle with the captain's breeches wreathed and festooned about his horse, industriously employed in trying to stretch and draw them back into a wearable shape. He reported progress to the captain's orderly (sent back frequently during the day with solicitous inquiries), and by the following morning, after cutting off about five feet from each trouser-leg, the captain was able to appear in attenuated and crinkled small-clothes, so tight and drawn that it was difficult to know whether it was breeches or nature that he wore.

About noon on August 23 Chalmers's cavalry division made an attack on our infantry outpost and met a disastrous defeat. The Seventh Kansas went out to reenforce, and, when the enemy was driven back, pursued him to the old battle-ground at Hurricane creek. Here a fight lasting over two hours took place, the enemy bringing a battery into action, but the regiment maintained its position until ordered back by General Hatch. Here was killed First Sergt. Alonzo Dickson, of company H. A braver man never lived nor one capable of more daring deeds.

On return to La Grange the regiment met orders to proceed immediately to St. Louis. It arrived there on September 17, 1864, and reported to General Rosecrans. It formed a part of the defense against Price, who was advancing north on his

last raid through Missouri. When Price turned west, the Seventh Kansas moved out in pursuit, while our forces were being concentrated to drive him from the state. When the troops were organized, the regiment was assigned to McNeil's brigade of Pleasanton's cavalry division. Skirmishing of more or less importance attended the advance across Missouri. On October 22 the enemy was struck at the Little Blue. He opened up with artillery, but was driven back on Independence, which place was captured by a brilliant cavalry charge. Two cannon complete and over a hundred prisoners were taken. Kansans must remember that the first sound of firing on Pleasanton's advance, that cheered their weary hearts and told them that relief was coming, was the thunder of the two cannon that played upon the Seventh Kansas as it charged in column up that long street through Independence, and, with Winslow, carried the Confederate position and captured the guns. Forty of the enemy's dead were left on the field. After an all-night march the Confederates were attacked near Hickman's Mills, the engagement lasting the entire day, the enemy retiring at nightfall, leaving his dead on the field. On the 25th, at the crossing of the Marmaton, the regiment participated in the cavalry charge that routed the Confederates; it also took part in the subsequent engagement at Shiloh creek, and indeed in all the battles of the pursuit.

From Newtonia, where the pursuit of Price was abandoned, the regiment returned across Missouri to the St. Louis district, where it was divided into detachments and stationed at various points. Guerrillas were quite active, especially around Centerville and Pattison, and the garrisons at these points had plenty to occupy their attention. Capt. Jim Smith swept Crowley's Ridge and sent over twenty to their long home in one day's action. John James,[7] a mere boy, a member of company D, killed the guerrilla leader, Dick Bowles, in open fight, the guerrilla having the decided advantage, being behind a fence with a Winchester, while the boy dismounted under fire and, kneeling in the open road, sent a bullet from his Spencer through the brain of the desperado. Dick Bowles was as conspicuous in his neighborhood as Bill Anderson used to be in

7. John James is now living at Olathe, Kan. His address was, last I knew, 413 South Cherry street, Olathe, Kan. It shows that all the James family were not rebels. John James came to Kansas with company D, made up in Bureau and Jo Davies counties, Illinois. His residence at enlistment was Wyanet. He came in as a recruit November 1, 1861; reenlisted as a veteran January 1, 1864, and was mustered out with the regiment September 29, 1865.

his. The headquarters of the regiment was at St. Louis during
the winter and until moved to Pilot Knob. Early in July,
1865, the companies were concentrated at Cape Girardeau,
and on July 18 moved by transports to Omaha, Neb. From
thence the regiment marched up the Platte to Fort Kearney,
and went into camp south of the trail to the southwest of the
fort.

The Seventh Kansas had fought its battles and its term of
service was drawing to a close, but its story would not be complete without a reference to two or three enlisted men who
bore a distinguished part in its history. There were a number
of men whose fund of humor was never exhausted and whose
bravery was always a subject of admiration. Conspicuous
among this class was Sergt. Morris Davidson, of company A,
familiarly known by his nickname, "Mot." His quaint jokes
are as fresh and funny to me to-day as they were twoscore
years ago. In 1861 the original pilot bread was issued to the
troops; it was modified later and an article of a less flinty
sort was issued; but the original article was something to be
remembered. It was soon after enlistment when Mot broke
a period of unusual silence, while the boys were at mess, with
the interrogative remark: "Boys, I was eating a piece of
hardtack this morning, and I bit on something soft; what do
you think it was?" "A worm," was the answer of the inevitable individual who stands ready with instant information.
"No, by G——," said Mot, "it was a tenpenny nail." Mot had a
deficiency in the roof of his mouth, and the defect in his
speech, like Charles Lamb's stutter, made his sayings seem
much funnier than they show up in cold print. He was absolutely fearless.

At Hurricane creek he was sent with four dismounted men
to scout across a gap between our left wing and center; a
similar gap existed in the enemy's line, and Mot crossed with
his men over the stream and crawled up around the left of
Chalmers's brigade, which opposed us. He opened fire on
their left rear from the brush, and the rebel leader, thinking
he was flanked, hastily withdrew his whole force and rapidly
fell back nearly a mile and formed a new line. As our line
advanced and took position across the stream, Davidson and
his men were met coming out of the brush, and then the cause
of Chalmers's retrograde movement, heretofore a matter of

mystery, became evident. "What on earth were you trying to do, sergeant?" was Colonel Herrick's remark, as he stared in astonishment at Mot and his diminutive army. "Trying to snipe 'em," was the sergeant's answer as he took his place in line. He had whipped a brigade. In the winter of 1862-'63, Mot was commanding a picket post of five men on Wolf river, in Tennessee. It was a bitter cold night, and, although the enemy was lurking about, Mot and his men had built a fire in a hollow and were huddled around it trying to keep from freez- ing, when they received a volley from the brush on the oppo- site side of the creek. "Twenty-five men with me and the rest hold horses!" thundered Mot as he dashed alone towards the enemy, who immediately fled.

Ira B. Cole, bugler of company H, familiarly known as "Buck" Cole, was another fellow of infinite jest. Colonel Herrick, who never changed expression or smiled when a funny thing was said, nevertheless appreciated a joke in his own way; he used to have Buck detailed as his bugler just to have him near, that he might hear his jokes, and Buck took advantage of 'the situation and played the court fool to his heart's content. He was notoriously sloven in his dress, but used to say "that he was bound to dress well if he did n't lay up a cent." He was not always amenable to discipline, and once, while he was carrying a log of wood up and down the company line as a punishment, was accosted by the chaplain, who had come for a book he had loaned Buck and had not been returned. The chaplain was a recent appointment, and as yet guileless, and when Buck suggested that he hold the log while he went after the book, the chaplain absent-mindedly took it, and, ten minutes later, when the captain appeared on the scene, was pacing up and down, thinking over his next Sun- day's sermon, with the stick still on his shoulder. Buck was found peacefully sleeping in his tent. He stated to the captain that he supposed the idea was to have the log carried, and as the chaplain was doing it he thought it would be all right.

There were those who made jokes, and those who enjoyed them, and conspicuous among the latter class was Elihu Hol- comb, of company A, known in common as "Boots." No mat- ter how serious and disarranged the surroundings, Boots always saw something to be amused at, and his mirthful laughter would ring out above the din and bring a smile to the face of despair. A marked occasion was at Coffeyville, when

the Confederates, after having been whipped and driven for many days, turned the tables on us and sent us back in retreat across the field to our rear. Boots deemed this to be an excellent joke, and during the retreat his laughter was easily distinguished between the crash of volleys, as he gave expression to his enjoyment.

I could go on and fill many pages with the humor that lived to temper the hardships of a soldier's life, and could relate instances of heroic daring that grew commonplace in their frequency. I have only referred to those instances which come uppermost in my mind as I write.

There was one incident that I would like to speak of, simple in itself, but it always left an impression on my mind that I never want to grow less distinct. When the Seventh Kansas entered Independence, Mo., the first time, in 1861, as it rode down the long street from Kansas City, toward the courthouse, to our left, a block away, two ladies stood on the upper floor of a double porch waving their handkerchiefs, loyal to the core. Three years later, when the regiment was charging up that same street against Price's artillery, which was sending shot and shell to meet it, those same two ladies stood on the same porch waving their handkerchiefs, and although we could not hear them, I know they were cheering.

The name "jayhawkers," given the regiment, was possibly a disadvantage, for it was this name that suggested to other regiments to lay their sins on our shoulders. It resulted in the regiment being declared outlaw by Confederate authorities, and a tacit understanding existed that, as far as the Seventh Kansas was concerned, no prisoners would be taken. Once Lieut. B. C. Sanders escorted some prisoners to a Confederate camp in Mississippi for exchange.[8] This was the

---

8. JAMES SMITH, of Topeka, was one of the squad with Captain Sanders on this occasion. James Smith was born in Armstrong county, Pennsylvania, July 29, 1837. He was the oldest son of Robert and Sarah (Wray) Smith. The mother died in 1860 and the father in 1892. The father and seven sons were in the Union army in the war of the rebellion—James, John, William, Matthew, Daniel, Elder, and Henry. Another, Robert, was on the plains freighting, while the ninth son, George, was too young. All the sons except James were in the Army of the Potomac. John was a prisoner at Andersonville, exchanged, and killed at Petersburg; Matthew died in the service, and William was severely wounded at Malvern Hill. James Smith was educated at Elder's Ridge Academy, Indiana county, and afterward graduated at Jefferson College, Pennsylvania. After graduation he taught school in Mississippi, and in 1860 emigrated to Kansas, settling in Marshall county. In 1861 he enlisted in company A, Seventh Kansas cavalry, serving as a private until 1864, when he reenlisted as a veteran. Upon his discharge, September 30, 1865, he resumed work on the farm. In 1865 he was elected a member of the house of representatives. In 1869 he was elected county clerk of Marshall county, reelected in 1871, holding for four years. In 1873 he was elected county treasurer, and reelected in 1875. Before the expiration of his second term he was nominated for secretary of state, in 1876.

ostensible purpose, but the real object was to locate and ascertain the strength of the rebel force. That night, in the rebel camp, under the softening influence of some excellent whisky that our squad had taken along, very cordial relations were established. A Confederate officer, growing frank in his discourse, finally declared that he stood ready to greet any Yankee under like circumstances, excepting one of those d—— Kansas jayhawkers; they were outlawed, and death was too good for them. Lieutenant Sanders, who never touched liquor, sat watching and taking notes. He smiled grimly, and in a few minutes, when asked what regiment he belonged to, quietly answered, "the Kansas jayhawkers." The situation looked a little dubious for a few moments, but the Confederates finally decided, in consideration of the excellent quality of the whisky, to make an exception in this instance, and cordial relations were reestablished. As soon as Sanders was out of the rebel camp the next morning on his return, he tore up the flag of truce, saying, "I don't want any white-rag protection; I 'll fight my way through from this time on." And he did. While the name "jayhawker" was a reproach among the white people of the South, it was a symbol of deliverance to the blacks, and in their simple minds a jayhawker was a Moses who would lead them out of bondage.

At Fort Kearney orders were received to proceed to Fort Leavenworth for final muster-out and discharge. "Assembly" was sounded at once and the order read to the men. In less than an hour thereafter camp had been struck and the regiment was moving down the river on its final march toward home. Fort Leavenworth was reached on September 14, and on the 29th of September, 1865, the companies formed on the parade-ground for the last time. They were formally mustered out, and the following day received their last pay and final discharge. Their tour of duty was ended.

He was reelected in 1878, and again in 1880, serving six years—through the administrations of John P. St. John and George W. Glick. He next served four years as private secretary to Gov. John A. Martin, following this with four years in the same capacity for Gov. Lyman U. Humphrey. During the receivership of the Atchison, Topeka & Santa Fe he was expert accountant for the master in chancery. He was appointed quartermaster-general of the state militia by Gov. William E. Stanley, which position he now holds. January 23, 1867, he was married to Miss Jane Edgar, of Marshall county. Capt. James Smith, of company C, was another person. Capt. B. C. Sanders is still living, in Cloud county, near Concordia, where he settled upon the close of the war. William H. Smith, a brother, has held various positions in Marshall county, and has been a member of the legislature several sessions. He was president of the State Historical Society for the year 1902. Five of the Smith brothers, James, William, Robert, Henry, and George, settled in Marshall county. James served for some time as quartermaster of the Seventh regiment.

I have called this "The Story of the Seventh Kansas," but
the story of the Seventh Kansas will never be written—can
never be written. The story of a few battles—not a tenth
part told; a sketch of many skirmishes—but briefly related,
are mere suggestions of four years of energetic action, of
hardship and suffering, and of gratification that strength had
been given to endure it all. I have not told the story of
marches under a midday sun that beat down and seemed to
shrivel up the brain as you gasp for breath in the dust beaten
up by the horses' feet; of marches through mud and never-
ceasing rain that soaked you, saturated you, until you felt
that you had dissolved into a clammy solution yourself; of
marches through winter storms of sleet and driving snow,
without hope of shelter or rest; of struggles against almost
irresistible drowsiness when sleep had been denied you for
days and to sleep now would be death; of weeks of tossing in
the fever ward of a field hospital, where the oblivion of stupor
came to you as a blessing; of thirsting for water when only
brackish, slimy pools festering in the sun were near to tan-
talize you—this part of the story has not been told. The thrill
and excitement of battle were wanting in all this; it was only
plain, monotonous duty, made endurable by the grim humor
that jeered at suffering and made a joke at the prospect of
death.

Winter or summer, a cavalry regiment in the field has no
rest. Picketing, patrolling, scouting, it is the eyes of the
army, and must not sleep. It leads the advance or covers the
rear; far away to the front, the infantry column, moving
along without interruption, hears the dull jar of cannon, or
the popping of carbines; it is the cavalry sweeping the road.
The fences torn down in gaps along the wayside indicate that
the enemy had grown stubborn and the cavalry had been deployed. A dismounted skirmisher can lie down and take advantage of cover; a mounted cavalryman is an easy mark for
a sharpshooter as he advances; but he must take his chances;
it is his duty. A cavalry regiment does not usually suffer a
heavy loss in any one engagement; it is one here, two or three
there—a constant attrition that is ever wearing away the
substance; it is the aggregate that tells the story. The dead
are scattered here and there, buried by the wayside where
they fell. Few have been gathered into the national ceme-
teries, but they rest as well, and the same glory is with them
wherever they may sleep.

The Early History of the Seventh Kansas Cavalry.

Written by S. M. Fox, late Adjutant Seventh Kansas Cavalry, for the Kansas State Historical Society.

TO INTERPRET history accurately and truthfully one must have lived as a part of the history of which he speaks. This is especially true as relates to the campaigns of the early Kansas regiments along the Missouri border during the first months of the civil war. Documentary evidence relating to these movements is exceedingly meager, and we cannot confidently rely on the ever-increasing exaggeration of tradition. Therefore, when one attempts to criticise certain traditionary acts he should make himself doubly sure of the ground on which he bases his criticism.

At this day, while some of the actors in the drama are still living, the need of the Kansas Historical Society is a statement of the facts based upon the personal knowledge of the narrator. His opinion of men with whom he has been thrown in intimate relationship in the past is of value. Their authenticated deeds he may well record; but great care should be taken that injustice be not done by a loose setting forth as fact that of which he has no personal knowledge, but which has come to him second-hand, through a possibly prejudiced source.

I have undertaken this article not to embalm any personal achievement, but to correct a misstatement so baseless that I would not feel justified in letting it go unchallenged. I will endeavor to be as impersonal as possible, but it will be necessary to inject the ego into this statement long enough to say that I was a member of the Seventh Kansas cavalry and served in its ranks continuously from its earliest beginning, in 1861, until the regiment was finally mustered out as a veteran organization, in the fall of 1865; and therefore speak from intimate personal experience, and am not required to gather my facts from any secondary source.

This article is inspired by the following statement taken from an article printed in the ninth volume of the "Kansas Historical Collections," under the title, "The Black-Flag Character of War on the Border," contributed by Henry E. Palmer, late captain in the Eleventh Kansas cavalry. I quote as follows:

"This demoralized, inhuman condition of affairs in the district of the border was not confined to one side. The Seventh Kansas cavalry, organized October 28, 1861, commanded by Charles R. Jennison, gained under Jennison's control a world-wide reputation as the 'Jayhawkers.' Returning from their first raid into Missouri, they marched through Kansas City, nearly all dressed in women's clothes, old bonnets and outlandish hats on their heads; spinning-wheels, and even gravestones, lashed to their saddles; their pathway through the country strewn with, to them, worthless household goods; their route lighted by burning homes. This regiment was little less than an armed mob until Jennison was forced to resign, May 1, 1862. As might be inferred, this man Jennison brought only disgrace to Kansas soldiery."

Captain Palmer reiterates the above lurid statement in the Kansas City

Star of November 24, 1908, in a reply to M. H. Madden, who had seen fit to take exceptions to some of Captain Palmer's statements in the above-quoted article. In this last communication to the *Star*, Captain Palmer goes on to strengthen his statement by saying:

"There are neighbors of Mr. Madden in your peaceful, prosperous city that have not forgotten this parade through your streets, which occurred about October 7, 1861."

I wish first to state here, before going further, that the Seventh Kansas cavalry (or the First Kansas cavalry, as it was then designated) never in its history paraded through Kansas City in the guise and manner depicted by Captain Palmer. It never "paraded through the streets of Kansas City . . . returning from its first raid into Missouri," nor returning from any other raid.[1]

It will be observed that Captain Palmer mixes his chronology. He has correctly given the date of the organization of the Seventh Kansas cavalry as October 28, 1861, but he later fixes the date of the alleged parade through Kansas City as October 7, 1861, twenty-one days before the regiment was organized.

It is a fact, however, that three companies of the Seventh Kansas were in Kansas City during the last half of September and the first half of October, 1861. These companies were, however, dismounted and without uniforms, having been rushed down from Fort Leavenworth to help defend the city against Price, then at Lexington. These companies made no raids whatever, but did provost duty, Major Anthony being provost marshal part of the time. Colonel Jennison had no rank in the regiment until the date of organization, October 28.[2] It was understood, of course, that he was to be the colonel. I was in Kansas City doing duty with one of the three companies, and it seems odd that I have no recollection of any parade made through Kansas City as described. I would certainly have been impressed with such a wild and wooly performance, as I was a tenderfoot not long out of the East. I do, however, have a very vague recollection of a story told in camp that Jennison had at one time marched defiantly through

NOTE 1.—Ex-Governor E. N. Morrill, of Hiawatha, a member of the Seventh Kansas, writes: "That story of Palmer's, it seems to me, is made up of whole cloth. It is absolutely false from beginning to end." From collateral incidents he fixes the date of the raid out to Independence as the 25th of November. The negroes of Independence had been waiting for the coming of a Moses, and Colonel Anthony was apparently the Moses that they were looking for, and they, doubtless following his suggestion, took wagons and carriages that they could find, loaded them with whatever they could gather up, and followed the regiment back to Kansas City, and the next day Anthony distributed the goods among the negroes and sent them over into freedom, which somewhere had an existence within the confines of Kansas. It is possible that the hazy memories of some of the old settlers have confused this negro hegira with the Seventh Kansas itself. The regiment went out and returned the same day in good order. I have no doubt this exodus of negro slaves was instigated by Anthony, and I think they went up to Leavenworth and trailed through the streets, seeking for homes in the promised land. Do you realize how much of the burning and alleged plundering in Missouri was done by the negroes, who took advantage of the conditions to even up old scores? Those negro slaves had an intelligence and knowledge of affairs beyond what many people realized. That day at Independence I remember that Colonel Anthony struck a man of company A over the head with his saber for being funny and putting on a woman's bonnet that he had picked up. Every regiment in the army had its complement of regimental fools that had to be suppressed.

Wilder's "Annals of Kansas" has the following: "December 20 (1861) One hundred contrabands freed by Colonel Anthony at Independence arrived at Leavenworth in gay procession." This freeing the slaves disturbed the rebel Missourians more than horse-stealing, or any other action of the Union troops.

NOTE 2.—While the governor had some weeks previously issued a commission to Charles R. Jennison as lieutenant-colonel, he was not mustered into the United States service until mustered colonel, October 28, 1861. D. R. Anthony was first commissioned as major, and was mustered such into the United States service on September 29, 1861. He was the recognized head of the

3

Kansas City with an independent company of his old Jayhawkers, but the memory is very indistinct.

There are no available records to fix the dates of many border incidents, but Jennison did range about with his independent company well into September, 1861, and it seems hard for many to separate its doings from the acts of the Seventh Kansas, later associated with Jennison's name.[3] Captain Palmer has fallen into this common error. It will doubtless be a surprise to the captain and others to learn that Colonel Jennison never for a minute commanded the Seventh Kansas in person on any raid or during any field operation in Missouri during the time he was connected with the regiment.

I never knew how or where Colonel Jennison spent a large portion of his time, or by what authority, other than his own, he was absent from his command. A part of his time was spent over the border in Kansas at a town known then as Squiresville. An occasional orderly—his means of communication with the regiment—would sometimes intimate that he was solacing the tedium of existence by an indulgence in a game of fascinating attraction in the West, known as draw-poker. Doubtless it was more attractive than the rude exercise that was necessarily an accompaniment of operations in the field. This is all that the rank and file knew of Jennison's whereabouts, and it was about all they cared. His influence on the regiment, if anything, was negative, and there were few who were not heartily glad when his wrath carried him to the precipitate step of sending in his resignation. This resignation was not forced, as Captain Palmer intimates, but was a voluntary act, induced by the appointment of James G. Blunt to the rank of brigadier-general, a position that he personally coveted and had hoped would be his. He made an intemperate speech to the men—the regiment was at Lawrence at the time—and during its course practically advised them to desert; and before his wrath cooled his resignation was out of his hands beyond recall. A few men, principally from company H (the company recruited by Cleveland), deserted in response to Jennison's advice. The number was not great, and doubtless some of them went to join the band that Cleveland was organizing at the time, and that later preyed for a brief season on Union man and rebel with just impartiality. Before I pass on I want to say that company H was never a disorderly organization. Cleveland resigned just as the regiment was organized, and his service with the company was practically nothing. It was always a fighting organization, and many of the best men in the regiment were in its ranks. The undesirable element had voluntarily eliminated itself.

In the sketch, "The Black-Flag Condition of the War on the Border," there seem to be many loose and inconsistent statements. Captain Palmer speaks frankly of the burning of Osceola, Mo., by his own command (Lane's

regiment until Jennison was mustered, as above. The regimental staff was organized in the middle of October, by the muster of John T. Snoddy (October 14, 1861) as adjutant, and, on the same date, Samuel Ayers as chaplain. It will be seen that the alleged ungodliness of the regiment was not due to the neglect of the governor in supplying an opportunity for religious training. Robert W. Hamer was mustered as quartermaster the following day and the regimental staff was supplied with a sequence of reports. Bibles and fodder.

NOTE 3.—Capt. W. E. Prince, Fort Leavenworth, to Gen. J. H. Lane, September 9, 1861: "I hope you will adopt early and active measures to crush out this marauding which is being enacted in Captain Jennison's name, as also yours, by a band of men representing themselves as belonging to your command."—War Records, vol. 3, series 1, p. 482.

brigade), and the big drunk indulged in by some of the troops that would have incapacitated them for defense had they been attacked that night. He mentions a drumhead court martial at Morristown, when seven prisoners were summarily condemned and shot to death as a retaliatory measure. Then, later, he makes this statement:

"The seventeen Kansas regiments, three batteries, and three colored regiments, with the exceptions above noted, gave the enemy no cause for guerilla warfare, but all left good records for brave and soldierly conduct, and the Seventh Kansas fully redeemed itself under Colonel Lee with Sherman's army, 1862 to 1864."[4]

The exceptions referred to were the Seventh and Fifteenth Kansas cavalry regiments.

I do not know the kind of meat that Cæsar has to feed upon to become an oracle. But the captain knew little or nothing of the redemption of the Seventh Kansas. Colonel Lee was a brigade commander, and did not personally command the regiment more than two months; and, besides, the Seventh Kansas never served in Sherman's army. Sherman was at one time a part of the army of the Tennessee, but the Seventh Kansas was never under him. I do not personally know anything relating to the Fifteenth Kansas cavalry, for I was serving far away, and the enemy confronting us was giving us sufficient to occupy our minds without worrying over other troubles. The men of the Fifteenth Kansas can make their own defense. However, I do protest against the name of Jennison being used to connect the Seventh Kansas with any event that occurred in Missouri.[5] Through two of its officers, Jennison and Cleveland, the regiment gained the name "Jayhawkers"—a heritage that brought trouble, but gave us the inspiration to make the name good.

Other statements of Captain Palmer, for the purpose of historical accuracy, call for correction. After giving a list of guerrilla chieftains who operated in western Missouri in the early part of 1861 and whose bloodcurdling war-cry was, "No surrender except in death!" he continues:

"The Kansans under Lane,[6] Montgomery, Blunt, Jennison, Anthony, Hoyt and others accepted the challenge, and until General Fremont, in October, 1861, issued his order against this retaliatory work and forced a reorganization of Lane's brigade, which forced Lane out of the army and back to the senate, there was no pretension to the common amenities of civilized war," etc.

It will be remembered, in an extract previously herein quoted, Captain Palmer states that, with the exception of the Seventh and Fifteenth Kan-

NOTE 4.—Maj. Charles G. Halpine, assistant adjutant-general to Secretary of War, March 14, 1862: "Nothing could exceed the demoralized condition in which General Hunter found the Third and Fourth Kansas infantry and Fifth and Sixth Kansas cavalry, formerly known as 'Lane's brigade,' on his arrival in this department. The regimental and company commanders knew nothing of their duties, and apparently had never made returns or reports of any kind."—War Records, vol. 8, series 1, p. 615.

NOTE 5.—There is an error in Coffin's "Settlement of the Friends in Kansas" (vol. 7, Kansas Hist. Col., p. 360). He says: The Seventh Kansas cavalry, Colonel Jennison's regiment, was made up about this time [1863] 1200 men. They obtained orders and crossed into Platte county, and with a besom of destruction, swept the border river counties, freeing all the slaves, of whom long cavalcades, with wagons, carriages, mules and stock, were crossing into Kansas continually." The date of this makes it clear that it was the Fifteenth Kansas, and not the Seventh. The Seventh was in Mississippi during the year 1863.

NOTE 6.—Senator P. B. Plumb once remarked to the secretary that Senator James H. Lane was the only man who commanded an army without a commission.

sas cavalry regiments, none of the Kansas organizations "gave the enemy cause for guerrilla warfare." The captain's statements do not seem to track. But, as to historical accuracy, note that he rings in Anthony and Hoyt in active connection with Lane, Montgomery, etc., before the issuance of Fremont's order in October, 1861, when the fact is that Anthony was not actively engaged in the field until November 11, and Hoyt was not yet in the service. While Hoyt was in service in Missouri with the Seventh Kansas he was an inconsequential second lieutenant; he became captain just as the regiment started for Mississippi, but until he resigned, not long after, he was for most part of the time in the sick squad, and cut no figure in the regiment worthy of mention.

In a list of lurid incidents, which the captain says "come before my mind as a panorama, vivid as life, a story that can never be told," etc., the following is mentioned as traveling by, among the other glaring scenes:

"Captain Charles Cleveland's desertion with several of company H, Seventh Kansas black-horse cavalry," etc.

History demands certain corrections: Cleveland's first name was Marshall, not Charles; the Seventh Kansas was never known as the "black-horse cavalry," but company H was for a brief time called the "black-horse company;" and, finally, Cleveland did not desert, but left the regiment regularly, by accepted resignation; also, the desertion of eight or ten men from company H was five months after Cleveland resigned. Otherwise the lurid vision is correct as relates to Cleveland.

I have been compelled to make the foregoing references to Captain Palmer's article to show that he was not sufficiently careful in verifying many of his statements, and that there is much chronological confusion, as frequently the act antedates its suggested cause. The story of the motley parade of the Seventh Kansas, led through Kansas City by Colonel Jennison, is pure fiction as far as the Seventh Kansas is concerned. Captain Palmer did not admire Colonel Jennison; nothing of good could therefore result from any connection with him, and, under the mistaken idea that Jennison was in active command of the regiment during its brief service in Missouri, it could be but a disorganized rabble, and it was safe to call it so He has failed utterly to discriminate between the lawless acts of Jennison, butting in with his independent company[7] along the border during the early months of the war, and the regiment which later was associated with his name.

As to the Seventh Kansas cavalry, Lieut.-Col. D. R. Anthony superintended the organization of the regiment and was the god of the machine. He was in active command of the regiment during the brief time it served in Missouri, and to him should be given all credit or blame that justly be-

NOTE 7.—Jennison was twice commissioned by Governor Robinson in the Kansas Militia in 1861, first on February 23, captain of Mound City Sharps Rifles Guards, and May 28, lieutenant-colonel Third regiment, southern division, Kansas Militia.
A correspondent in the Leavenworth *Conservative*, writing from Fort Scott, July 10, 1861, and signing himself "Jayhawker," tells of the operations of Captain Jennison in Missouri. Starting from Mound City, July 4, with thirteen men, he entered Vernon county, Missouri, July 5, and organized a company of forty-five men, with Isaac Morris, of Vernon county, Missouri, captain. Recruits from both states came in rapidly. Another company, under Ben Rice, soon joined the first, when separately they raided several secession camps, capturing army supplies, horses, etc., among them an ox-train with military supplies for Fort Arbuckle. Although Captain Jennison was not known as an officer, all recognized him as commander-in-chief of the expedition, which reached Fort Scott with 800 recruits. His purpose, it is stated, was to pass down through southwest Missouri and cooperate with United States troops in protecting Union men. —Colonel Jennison's Scrap-book, vol. 1, p. 11.

longs to this organization growing out of its service along the border. This service began about November 10, 1861, and ended January 31, 1862. Two weeks of this time was spent in camp up in Kansas, south of Leavenworth, and therefore its service in Missouri was of little more than two months' duration. Regiments had been marched to and fro. Lane's brigade of four regiments had been in the field for several months, moving up and down the border. Internecine strife was continuous with the people themselves, and when the Seventh Kansas first came into Missouri the desolate monuments that marked the destruction of barns and dwellings were to be seen with pitiful frequency; and yet it is fashionable to charge this desolation to the regiment that became heir to the name of "Jayhawkers." What this regiment actually did is sin enough, but it was a very small part when compared with the whole.

The statement that "With the exception of the Seventh and Fifteenth Kansas cavalry, there were no better disciplined or better behaved troops in the Union army than the Kansas men," is a very extravagant phrase. The Kansas regiments were rushed into service before they were half organized. None of them were well disciplined at the beginning, and many incompetent officers were at first selected. It took time to get rid of incompetency, and the governor did much harm in commissioning inexperienced men from civil life and sending them out to take places that men who had made good by efficient service were justly entitled to. The two first regiments were magnificent organizations, but they received their discipline on the bloody field of Wilson Creek.[8] The sobering influence of a desperate battle will accomplish more in a day towards discipline than the martinet can bring about in a year of strenuous effort. None of the regiments at the first held the edge over the others, as far as discipline went. No state certainly had the variety of adventurous material that made up the Kansas organization. There were Puritans and "hellions," and the intermediate grades of men; some praised God, and others cursed in His name; but they all were from a race militant, and, whether disciplined or not, fought when the chance offered.

When the Seventh Kansas was paraded for muster at Fort Leavenworth on the date of the organization, October 28, 1861, but nine companies were in line. Company K, which Capt. John Brown, jr., was recruiting in Ohio had not reached the state. Jennison appeared in person for the first time, and, after getting himself "balled up" while trying to put the regiment through the manual of arms, rode away and left the command to Lieutenant-Colonel Anthony. I do not recall having seen Colonel Jennison again with the regiment until at Humboldt in February, 1862, where he was stationed in command of a brigade. If he visited the regiment at any time while in Missouri, it was a transient call. Colonel Anthony was permitted to exercise his own will without check or hindrance, so far as any apparent interference by Jennison was concerned. What that will was, Colonel Anthony has been too recently with us and is too well known to make a statement nec-

NOTE 8.—In the battle of Wilson Creek the First Kansas lost fifty-one per cent. of those engaged in killed and wounded. At the time of this battle the First and Second Kansas had been in the service but two months. During the battle Major Sturgis remarked to General Lyon,. "These Kansas boys are doing the best fighting that I ever witnessed." The First regiment afterwards traveled 6000 miles, through eight rebel states. The Second regiment was the last one to leave the field (Wilson Creek), and the only regiment which kept its line and organization unbroken from the first to the last of the fight, which lasted about six hours.

essary. The reader's judgment would doubtless be nearer the mark than Colonel Anthony's own, for he stated at a state editorial meeting a few years ago, while in a reminiscent mood, that he felt the greatest mistake he had made in life was, he had been too conservative.

When about the middle of October, 1861, the three companies returned from Kansas City to Fort Leavenworth, as is stated earlier in this paper, clothing and equipment began to be issued. An unmustered company came from Illinois on escort duty, and they were persuaded to remain and cast their fortune with Kansas; they became company D. Finally, on October 28, nine companies being organized, and company K just ready to start from Ohio under young John Brown, the complete organization was accomplished.

Jennison, as I have said, appeared for a brief moment; and it was just about this time that the thrilling scene that preceded Cleveland's resignation was enacted. A dismounted parade had been formed on the "blue-grass," Colonel Anthony receiving the salute. Cleveland had made his first appearance. He was dressed in a somewhat motley garb—a soft hat, a regulation coat, drab trousers thrust into low-topped riding-boots, a belt carrying a surplus of revolvers and a saber that seemed a hindrance. Colonel Anthony did not approve of the drab trousers, and forthwith proceeded to deliver a public censure; whereupon the restive Jayhawker proceeded to advance to the "front and center" without waiting for orders. There was language, profane and incisive, while each man looked the other directly in the eye. The amenities being passed, they glared at each other a moment, then Cleveland, with a parting compliment which has passed down into history, strode away to his horse, hitched near by, and a moment later was galloping toward Leavenworth city. His resignation quickly followed, and was as promptly accepted.

Men of the class of Jennison and Cleveland were nothing if not spectacular. Jennison while colonel of the Seventh Kansas never wore the regulation head-gear; he always affected a tall, brimless fur cap. I recall my first vision of Cleveland. I was an eastern tenderfoot, and was being inducted into a knowledge of the new western world by a much-experienced brother recruit. We were sauntering down Shawnee street in Leavenworth, and had just stopped to read a newly posted bill. It was headed "Reward," and beneath it was set forth that a tempting number of dollars would be handed over to the individual who would bring in the body of one Marshall Cleveland, "dead or alive." We had both concluded that we were not hard up, and had started down the street, when we saw a gentleman with a neatly trimmed black beard riding towards us up the street. He was neatly dressed in a drab suit, low riding boots and a soft hat gracefully slouched. He wore the universal belt, and a bulge on either side in the tails of his frock coat made it plain to see that he was not defenseless. His horse looked like a thoroughbred, and he seemed wonderfully at home in the saddle. I remarked: "That's a mighty fine horse." My friend answered: "It ought to be; he has the pick of Missouri. That's Cleveland." Nobody offered to arrest him, and he rode on up the street. He went south on Fifth, and turned east on Delaware street. He was offering his person to the reward-seekers with a reckless nonchalance that thrilled my unsophisticated nature to the core. I, however, did not hover in his vicinity.

8

The same evening while I—still inducted by my guide—was listening with curiosity rather than delight to the much-bedazzled prima donna of the slums, at the "Moral Show" that stood by the old market-house at the corner of Fifth and Shawnee streets, a little flurry brought attention to the fact that Cleveland was leaning against a post in the back part of the hall. He nodded to a few acquaintances, refused the request of a cross-eyed Hebe to invest in her liquid wares, and presently sauntered out. My next information was that the offer of reward had been withdrawn, and that Cleveland had been authorized to recruit a company for Jennison's regiment.

The organization of the Seventh Kansas being effected, the regiment, well uniformed, well mounted, but indifferently armed, moved down through Kansas to Kansas City and went into camp. Anthony, in person, with companies A, B and H, went into bivouac on the Majors farm, about four miles southeast of Westport. The remainder of the regiment, except company K, camped in nearer to Kansas City, on O. K. creek. ·

It will be remembered that all of the city practically lay north of the junction [Main and Delaware] in those days, and did not reach out very far to the east or west. The McGee division, to the south, contained a brick block of three or four stores and a few scattering houses and was connected with the city by an unpaved road, unless six inches of Missouri clay mud can be called a pavement.

It is not necessary to keep harping about the conditions that prevailed along the Kansas border at this time, yet possibly a little retrospection may make matters plainer to those who were not participants in these affairs. The border-ruffian element in Missouri had held the ascendency during 1855 and 1856, and rode over Kansas roughshod. They had burned Lawrence and Osawatomie, and plundered other hamlets; had committed murders and outrages through the settlements, and had shown no mercy. Montgomery and John Brown, who were essentially men of action, began to lead their followers to resistance, and others followed their lead. There were others who rode up and down and raged, but made little show of accomplishment. The steady northern persistence finally made itself felt, and the border-ruffian element was gradually thrown on the defensive. They had sown the wind and the whirlwind had to be reaped.

When the war became a fact, the conditions along the Kansas border were unlike anything elsewhere. There were bitter wrongs to be righted, and no one can stay the power of revenge. The creed of self-repression, where the reversed cheek is to be submitted to the smiter, finds but few who will accept it in times of stress. They rather turn to the Old Testament, where a contrary doctrine can find support. John Brown had become a martyr, and his soul militant had commenced its march of freedom, and inspired feet were swinging into step to follow. Loyal Missourians, driven from their homes, had joined the Union army, with the bitter purpose to accomplish reprisal and revenge. No one can make a comparison with conditions existing anywhere else in the land. The situation must be judged by itself; it can admit of no comparison; it stands unique and alone.

Imagination doubtless depicts the "Jayhawkers," represented in the individuals who made up the Seventh Kansas cavalry, as bearded desperadoes with mustaches painted and drooping and a bellicose swagger that suggested trouble to the timorous wayfarer. The truth is that a majority

of this regiment were beardless youths. Some of them had roughed it through life and were coarse of fiber, but many others had come from cultured homes in New England and Eastern states. Not half of the regiment was recruited in Kansas, but there was leaven enough to permeate the lump. One company was recruited in Ashtabula county, Ohio, organized by a son of John Brown, and did not need any leavening influence. Three whole companies and the halves of two others came from Illinois. The John Brown company came the long journey that the name of "Kansas" might be associated with their efforts toward the overthrow of slavery. They were saturated with the spirit of the martyrs. As to education, the men ranked high above the average. The regiment furnished more clerks at the various headquarters than any other similar organization in the Sixteenth army corps. The men were not ruffians or desperadoes, but averaged fairly with other regiments of the civil war. They were probably no better or no worse. [9]

The name of "Jayhawker" was not an asset at first to be highly valued. The men laughed at it and accepted it. They did not realize what might happen to them in future ages when the ambitious historian turned his imagination loose on the iniquities that attended the name. When, in the spring of 1862, the regiment was ordered down to the Army of the Tennessee, where real war was on tap, the name suggested a scapegoat, and every regiment in the army corps began systematically to lay their depredations on the shoulders of the Seventh Kansas. We had our pay held up for over eight months because we refused to make good the depredations committed almost entirely by an Illinois regiment. It was for this injustice that the First Kansas, out of sympathy (God bless them!), refused to cheer General Grant when so ordered, as they marched by his headquarters at Oxford, Miss., in the fall of 1862. And this grand old regiment was mighty well disciplined, too. I love this old regiment. We served together for almost a year. I never shall forget the scene at the Tallahatchie when the rebels began their advance toward our little regiment from their forts along the bottom. Forty siege-guns were filling the atmosphere with bursting shells, and things looked dubious. But just then the infantry column came up at double time, the First Kansas in the advance—"Jayhawkers, ye'll have help now!" All hell couldn't have taken that hill.

During the summer of 1862 the Seventh Kansas served under the great cavalry leader, General Sheridan, then a colonel, at Rienzi, the extreme southern outpost of the army. The service was hazardous and exacting, but this efficient soldier often spoke in generous praise of the service rendered. During the advance of General Grant's army down the Mississippi Central Railway toward Vicksburg in the fall of 1862, day after day the Seventh Kansas held the post of honor as the advance-guard of the main infantry column, and it skirmished and fought over every foot of the way between the Cold Water and Coffeyville. It cleared and carried the crossing of every intermediate stream; charged through and captured Holly Springs in the early morning, with military stores and many prisoners; charged the rebel battery at Waterford and captured one of its guns; and finally drove

NOTE 9.—The American Bible Society had a depository at Harrisonville, Mo. When a detachment of the Seventh Kansas entered the town the store had been already looted by some previous organization, but the Bibles were left intact. The Seventh Kansas took the Bibles. It might be pleasant at this late date for the Bible Society to learn that their involuntary charity had been so appropriately applied.

the enemy behind their breastworks at the Tallahatchie, and held them there for eight hours until the infantry advance came up, led by the grand old First Kansas infantry. These eight hours were passed under the steady fire of forty siege-guns that made up the Confederate batteries. Men of the Seventh Kansas crawled that night through the rebel pickets and into their fortifications, and brought the news that the enemy were evacuating. In the early morning this regiment forced a crossing and followed, harassing their rear-guard from Abbeyville to Oxford, and, driving back their artillery, carried the town by a charge, fighting every inch of the way through the streets. Between the Tallahatchie and Water Valley this one regiment captured over 2000 prisoners. At Coffeyville, where the entire cavalry division was led into a trap by an inefficient leader, the Seventh Kansas was in the brunt of the battle, and fell back in order, and it was the Seventh Kansas that formed at the Tillaboba bridge against the rebel infantry and stopped their pursuit. General Grant never criticised the fighting qualities of the regiment.

Gen. G. M. Dodge, when in command of the Sixteenth army corps, always gave the Seventh Kansas cavalry the preference, and plainly told us so. While under his command the Seventh Kansas and Tenth Missouri cavalry (Cornyn's brigade), numbering less than 1000 men, whipped to a finish 3500 men under Roddy at Leighton, Ala., and a week later the augmented brigade whipped General Gholson's army at Tupello, Miss., capturing an entire regiment of Confederate cavalry.

During the campaigns of Gen. A. J. Smith against Forrest, in northern Mississippi, in 1864, that splendid fighter detached the Seventh Kansas from the cavalry corps, and the Jayhawkers were again given the honored position of advance-guard of the main infantry column. It cleared the way from the north line of Mississippi to Pontotoc; and when Smith made a feint retreat to maneuver Forrest outside of his fortifications, the Seventh Kansas fought for sixteen hours, covering the rear against Forrest's entire cavalry division. Only those who have been up against Forrest know what this means. Forrest himself says, referring to this rear defense: "He took advantage of every favorable position, and my artillery was kept almost constantly busy." The whole wagon-train for the most of the day had but the Seventh Kansas between it and the enemy's cavalry. General Smith's confidence in the regiment must have been great; and it was not mistaken— not a wagon was lost.

The above incidents are cited to show that under great war leaders the Jayhawkers were trusted and honored, and that as a fighting regiment it always made good. It fought an offensive warfare, not waiting to be attacked, but dashed in and got in that effective first blow that wins the fight. Even during its two months in Missouri in the winter of 1861-'62, its killed and wounded was almost fifty per cent. more than the similar loss in Lane's brigade during the whole time it was under Lane's command.

The first movement made into Missouri, as has been said, was by companies A, B and H, led by Colonel Anthony. On the evening of November 10, 1861, a loyal Missourian came in with the information that the rebel Up. Hayes had assembled his band of guerrillas for mischief, and was in camp on the Little Blue about thirteen miles out. Anthony immediately moved, with 110 men, and after an all-night march attacked the rebel camp at early

morning of the 11th. A desperate fight followed. The rebel force greatly outnumbered Anthony's command, but, taken by surprise, they were driven from their camp with heavy loss, and their horses, wagons and entire camp equipment were captured. The guerrillas retreated to the bluffs and rallied behind the rocks in a strong defensive position, from which they could not be driven. Our loss was nine men killed and about thirty wounded, many of the latter, however, but slightly. The rebel dead left in camp was a much larger number. Anthony retired, bringing away all his killed and wounded and all the captured property. The writer was, with the reënforcements, hurried out to Anthony's support. He was met some eight miles out, on his return march. There were farm-wagons and bed-quilts, a part of the primitive rebel equipment. In some of the wagons were the severely wounded, stolidly bearing their pain; in others the bed-quilts covered motionless shapes, and told the pitiful story of death and sacrifice. There were no "women's dresses," nor "spinning-wheels" nor "gravestones strapped[10] to the horses"—the gravestones were a matter for after-consideration. This was the first raid of the Seventh Kansas into Missouri.

Soon after the regiment went into camp together on the Westport road, near the old McGee tavern. From this camp the regiment made a march out to Independence, returning the same day. This movement is called "a raid" by Britton in his "Civil War on the Border, 1861-'62," (page 176). He erroneously fixes the date in September (more than a month before the Seventh Kansas was organized), and credits the speech in the court-house square to Jennison. Jennison was not present; Colonel Anthony was in command and made the speech.

When Price retreated south from Lexington he promised to soon return with reënforcements and occupy the country permanently. The rebel sympathizers around Independence were aggressively elated, and the spirit of secession blatantly rampant. Threats were being made against loyal citizens, and many were being driven from their homes and compelled to come over into Kansas for safety.

Both the march out and return were orderly. It was not the first time Union troops had passed over this road. Some destroying hand had sometime preceded us; along the road were several lonely chimneys and blackened remains of houses. As we entered Independence, riding down the long, sloping street to the business part of the town, we saw two ladies waving their handkerchiefs from the upper floor of a double porch, at the rear of a house about a block to the left. When we returned in the afternoon they were again at their post. Three years later, when the veteran Seventh Kansas had been rushed by forced marches from Mississippi to help defend Kansas against Price, and as the extreme advance of Pleasanton's relieving army charged up that same street against a battery in action on the crest, two ladies were waving their handkerchiefs from that same porch.

NOTE 10.—The writer of this article has had some experience with pack-trains, but is at a loss just how to proceed to strap a spinning-wheel to a saddle, especially as the saddle is to be occupied by a rider. The statement seems a little extravagant. Also, the setting of the scene seems to be a little contradictory. That the route should be "lighted by burning homes" requires a background of darkness, and that the particulars of the fantastic garb and impedimenta alleged to have been borne by the recreant Jayhawkers be made evident, the light of day would seem to have been most necessary. Also, referring to the "gravestones" that were strapped to the saddles, might they not have been finger-boards taken from the crossroads? Or perhaps the word "gravestones" is a misprint for grindstones; for it was the universal custom of the Seventh Kansas to take possession of all grindstones found along the line of march. These were worn on the watch-chain as an ornament or fob.

12

Shells were bursting and bullets were flying thick, but they maintained their post to the end. They did not seem to have any grudge against the Seventh Kansas.

While at Independence the regiment was not permitted to break ranks. The male citizens were rounded up and corraled in the court-house square, and Colonel Anthony, from the court-house steps, impressed upon their minds some wise and salutary truths. I do not know that much good was accomplished, but I am sure Colonel Anthony himself must have been greatly relieved when he got that red-hot stuff out of his system. No houses were burned at any time. The regiment made an orderly march back to their camp and did not parade through Kansas City, and the lurid story of the route being "lighted by burning homes" lacked the necessary background of darkness to have made it effective.

Colonel Anthony was a rigid disciplinarian and exacted obedience on every occasion. He was at times tyrannical, and on several occasions he stood perilously near death when he threatened men with the flat of his saber. He never stood for foolishness, and while on the march was constantly up and down the column watching the conditions, and if the fool of the regiment had deemed it funny to array himself in any grotesque manner he would have been ordered to dismount and continue the rest of the march on foot, and when in camp the most unpleasant part of fatigue duty would have been assigned to him. No culprit could ever hope to escape through forgetfulness: his case was always attended to. The army was too new for this excess of discipline, and often he would have accomplished more by less exacting methods. He was himself restive under authority, and did not hesitate to express his opinion of the incompetency of certain officers over him, and this was not a good pattern of discipline to set for his men. The first year of the war was a great strain on the army. A lot of incompetent book soldiers had to be tried out, and the great leaders were yet subordinates, who had still to make themselves evident by their works. In the regiment, the first selection of company officers was not always a success. They were elected by the men. But I will say this method produced better results than would have obtained from a direct independent appointment by the governor; and this opinion is abundantly sustained by the character of the appointments he later imposed upon us from civil life. Two of his appointments did make good. Capt. Jacob M. Anthony illustrated the Kansas motto, but he was helped by peculiar conditions; and Fred Emery, the other, very soon was transferred to the regimental staff as adjutant, and did not have a disgruntled company of men behind him to make life a tantalizing and troublous journey. All the rest went down to oblivion through forced resignation or the sentence of a court martial.

A few days after this "raid" out to Independence, the Seventh Kansas moved out by a roundabout way to Pleasant Hill. On this march guerrilla pickets were in evidence on distant elevations, disappearing over the crest whenever a near approach was made. Late in the morning a heavy fog came down, and the advance was necessarily very cautious. When the fog suddenly lifted, the point, consisting of six men under the command of First Sergt. Johnny Gilbert of company C, saw a squad of men grouped up the road near a house on a hill. He immediately charged, and the guerrillas, evidently thinking the whole regiment was behind the yells that the six

throats were emitting, broke and wildly stampeded down the road, and, to
the surprise of the charging squad, about eighty mounted men, who had
been invisible behind an echelon of barns and stacks, dashed out and, terror-
stricken, followed them.   One dead mule and one wounded prisoner were
the material fruits of this unexpected victory.   I cannot refrain from inject-
ing here an item of personal achievement.   I charged with this squad, but I
could not help it—my horse ran away.   As to Johnny Gilbert, he later deserted, leaving all government property carefully scheduled behind him in
his tent.   He had been outraged by the appointment by the governor of an
incompetent, cowardly civilian to a commissioned vacancy that in all justice
belonged to him.   I saw him later in the service as a sergeant of artillery
in a famous battery attached to the Sixteenth army corps.

A few days later the regiment came back and went into camp in the old
fair-ground at Independence.   While at this camp fifteen picked men were
sent out, under command of Lieut. Frank Ray, to the north as far as the
river.   A written list of about a dozen houses, scatteringly located, was
given him, with verbal instructions to burn them.   This was systematically
done.   Ray had been a sergeant in the regular army.   His force was small
and the neighborhood was full of danger, and he kept his men compactly
together.   No looting was permitted, not even from houses burned.   One
old Roman matron helped the destruction by throwing a pillow-case a quarter
full of powder in her fireplace, and walked from the ruins apparently un-
scathed.   Whether the orders for this burning came from higher than regimental authority I never knew.   There was no row made at Fort Leavenworth
over it, as was the case in subsequent events.

The regiment went north into Kansas for about two weeks, being during
the time in camp about eight miles south of Leavenworth.   On December
10 the Seventh Kansas was ordered to West Point, in the northern part of
Bates county, Missouri.   There was no town there at the time, it having
been burned by other vandals than the Jayhawker regiment.   On December
24, the regiment marched north in the face of a blinding blizzard, to Morristown, or where Morristown[11] had once stood.   This town was also little more
than a name; the anticipatory torch had some time before blotted it out.   It
was here that Col. Hampton Johnson of the Fifth Kansas cavalry had been
ambushed and slain at the crossing of the stream, in September; and it was
here, I believe, at that time, that seven Confederate prisoners were subjected to the action of a drumhead court martial and shot at the edge of their
graves.   The justice of this act does not concern the history of the Seventh
Kansas.   It occurred before the service of that regiment began.   This was
the permanent camp of the regiment during the remainder of its stay in
Missouri.

On the last day of 1861 a raid was made out to Dayton and Rose Hill.
The latter town was in the southeast corner of Johnson county.   Fulkerson,
Scott and Britty, rebel officers, were recruiting through this neighborhood.
Many Union families were being driven out and over into Kansas, and
brought stories of burning and outrage to our camp.   There was much skir-

NOTE 11.—A correspondent signing himself "A. B. M.," writing from near Morristown, July
23, 1861, speaks of the capture of Morristown, Mo., July 22, by Captain Jennison with twenty-five
of his own men and twenty volunteers.   Two wagon-loads of "contraband" goods were taken
and distributed through the camp.   To the writer's share fell two hats, a necktie, drawers,
bridle-bit, soap, pencils, blank books, writing-paper, and, as company steward, a supply of drugs
and medicines.—Jennison Scrap-books, vol. 1, p. 13.

14

mishing during this trip, and Colonel Anthony was in personal command.[12]
The town of Dayton was burned by his order, and he never shrank from the
responsibility. Scattering farmhouses were also burned, and doubtless
horses were taken and some looting done. Anthony made a report of this
expedition. His action was disapproved by General Hunter, and he was
censured, but never punished.

I cannot speak personally of the occurrences during the month of January, 1862, for I passed that month in an old remnant of a house at Morristown set apart for a hospital. The delirium of typhoid fever blotted out
my memory during that time. I can say, however, that there was much
fighting during that month, and the regiment lost seven or eight men killed
in action, and a number of men were wounded. On January 9 an expedition
was made, under Major Herrick, to Holden and Columbus. Company D
was ambushed at the latter place and driven back. Captain Utt, with company A, captured the town, buried our dead and burned the village. There
was much scouting during the remaining time in Missouri. Horses were
brought in, and doubtless many found their way to private homes in Kansas, and not many to the government corrals. It has been said that Jennison profited by the sale of some of them; but it is better understood that
his active coöperator, when he resigned and sold this stock, told Jennison to
whistle for his share.

Jennison evidently directed operations from a distance, in a limited sense,
and a very limited portion of the command was involved. It is to be remembered that the desertions from company H were a matter of subsequent
history. The regiment, as a body, was under a reasonable state of discipline. On January 31, 1862, the Seventh Kansas started on its march to
Humboldt, Kan., which town had been burned during the previous October by
rebel raiders led by Col. Talbott. Missouri knew the Seventh Kansas no more
until the Price raid of the fall of 1864 brought back that regiment by forced
marches from Mississippi. The hurried rush up the river to St. Louis from
Memphis, the day-and-night march across Missouri, and the charge at Independence were subsequent history. The firing in the rear of Price's army,
that told the almost exhausted Union soldiers at Kansas City that relief had
come, was directed at the charging Kansas regiment, that had outlived
obloquy and come into its heritage.

There is a good deal of rot connected with the theory that any especial
man or deed was responsible for the raid on Lawrence. The original burning of Lawrence, Osawatomie, etc., was responsible for Montgomery, Jennison, etc., and the campaigns along the border in 1861 held the Missouri

NOTE 12.—The rebels in Jackson county never fought unless they had the advantage; they
laid in ambush and bushwhacked. They did not wear uniforms, but wore citizens' clothing, and
when cornered hid their guns and came out whining that they were Union men. Whenever a
house was burned they always sent up a howl about being "Union," when no house was burned
unless it was well-known that the owner was a guerrilla and out in the "bresh." The only howl
made was by "Grandmother" Halleck, and General Hunter, who learned better later. In Alabama
we went out and burned and destroyed barns, corn and fodder, and brought away all horses and
mules; also cattle, as a rebel brigade made this their home and came out to raid upon our outly-
ing camps. Whenever a train was fired upon by guerrillas we immediately destroyed all buildings and property within a radius of several miles. We burned Oxford, Miss., in retaliation for
the burning of Chambersburg, Pa., by Early. (We got the news from a rebel newspaper which
was exulting over it.)
Order of General Grant to General Sheridan, August 16, 1864: "If you can possibly spare a
division of cavalry, send them through Loudon county to destroy and carry off the crops, ani-
mals, negroes, and all men under fifty years of age capable of carrying arms," etc.
This destruction was common throughout the army. It was a necessity. When Grant fell
back from Oxford, Miss., in the winter of 1861 and 1862, we covered the rear. Fences, barns and
houses were burning, destroyed by the infantry column in advance of us.

guerrillas in check for the time. Quantrill was a moral degenerate, and when one follows the subsequent career of train-robbing and murder of Jesse James, Cole Younger and others of Quantrill's old gang, the question of inducement to slaughter seems to be a superfluity.. Quantrill doubtless had his eyes on Lawrence from the beginning, and was only watching for a propitious season to carry out a long-matured plan.

As to the conditions in Missouri after the Seventh Kansas left, the following extract from a letter of O. G. Cates, of Jackson county, Missouri, to Hon. E. M. Stanton, Secretary of War, bearing date of February 26, 1862, (War Records, vol. 17, part 2, p. 93) will illustrate:

"It now appears that, although the Kansas volunteer troops in obedience to orders did leave the state of Missouri, the substituted United States troops in that county (Jackson) have made no change in their mode of warfare for the better; the same wanton and lawless violation on the rights of private property have continued without check or hindrance. Bands of negroes, slave and free, and clans of white men, thief and Jayhawker, from the state of Kansas, with the knowledge of the United States forces thus substituted, are permitted in open day to enter our county and freely gratify their savage lust of plunder and private revenge on defenseless and terror-stricken people."

It would appear from the above that the Seventh Kansas was not responsible for all the wrongs on the border.[13] The Seventh Kansas had become heir to the name "Jayhawkers," and they bore it to the end. The regiment was neither an aggregation of devils nor saints. The regiment did always fight well, and gained some honor. Propitious fate transferred them to the Army of the Tennessee, and their initial service there was directly under Col. Philip Sheridan. Without orders, the regiment charged General Price's camp at Marietta, Miss., and rode through it and brought away his headquarters flag, and would have burned the camp had not Sheridan in person ordered us to withdraw. The Seventh Kansas rode down through Funderberger's Lane in the night against an unknown foe, and routed a superior force. The Seventh Kansas, unaided and far from support, charged Jackson's veteran cavalry division of over 4000 men, and the lane at Lamar was strewn with rebel dead. Thirty-six killed, 500 prisoners, hundreds of horses and over 2000 stands of arms were the fruits of this victory. The infantry regiments came out and cheered us as we passed their camps on our return, and it became a custom that obtained for months

NOTE 13.—A careful reading of the war records of operations in Jackson and surrounding counties during 1862, between the time that the Seventh Kansas was withdrawn and the "Red Leg" service began—that houses of rebels continued to be burned by Union troops, as is noted in the reports of Col. John T. Burris and others (War Records, vol. 8), and the "capture" of horses by the hundreds that were seized and brought out of Missouri, which are mentioned in these reports—indicate that the warfare of 1861 continued, and it does not appear that any specific censure emanated from headquarters. Also Gen. Ben. Loan, on November 17, 1862, assessed $15,000 against the disloyal citizens of Jackson county, $7500 to be applied to subsist enrolled militia, and $7500 for destitute families of soldiers engaged in active service. General Curtis alone seemed to comprehend the situation, as his communication to General Loan (War Records, vol. 13, p. 688), dated September 29, 1862, indicates:
". . . You think Lane and Jennison should be sent to a 'safe place.' I think it would be safe to send them against the rebels and Indians that are now collected and invading McDonald, Barry and Stone counties. But let terror reign among the rebels. It will be better to have them under such power than loose to carry on guerrilla warfare which drives good people out of Jackson and Lafayette. . . . What rights have the rascals that go skulking about in the garb of citizens, not soldiers? Even our enrolled militia go with a badge on their hats; but these bands of so-called 'Partisan Rangers' sneak through the brush with no emblems of war, but with the stealthy, concealed garb of a private citizen, seek to continue the business of stealing, robbing and murdering. They deserve no quarter, no terms of civilized warfare. Pursue, strike and destroy these reptiles, and report to these headquarters as often as possible."
On the date that General Curtis wrote this characteristic letter the Seventh Kansas was hanging on the flank of Van Dorn's army, advancing on Corinth, and attacked their train at Bone Yard.

after. We began to feel that we could eventually trot in the same class with the old First Kansas infantry, which was among the cheerers. It is an old story and has been briefly told elsewhere. As time went on the name "Jayhawkers" lost its opprobrium, and the Seventh Kansas began to make it an honorable appellation. Yet it was the same regiment, little changed from the band which had served about two months in Missouri, and, if we believe vague tradition, laid the country desolate.

Cleveland met his fate as a discredited outlaw at the ford of the Marais des Cygnes. Jennison has cashed in his checks, withdrawn from the turbulent game of life, and judgment has been passed upon him. With all his sins, he had a gambler's generosity, and he often made life endurable to some poor struggling soul. May his deeds of kindness be remembered and all that was evil in his nature be forgotten.

Let us see. Kansas aspires to be called the "Jayhawker State." Our most illustrious citizens hail the name as a badge of honor. Our great University perpetuates the name in its war-cry that celebrates victory or shouts defiance after stubborn defeat. How came dishonor to be purified? Did not that one cavalry regiment that inherited the name and bore it through four years of strenuous war do much to make it what it is? How else was the miracle accomplished?

CPSIA information can be obtained
at www.ICGtesting.com
Printed in the USA
LVHW080848210323
742068LV00034B/1175